THE
people's
PRESIDENT

THE
people's
PRESIDENT

What a **Mom, Survivor** *and*
National Radio Talk Show Host
would do to **Fix** *the* **Country**

Dr. Laurie Roth

Keylite PSI

Keylite PSI

PO Box 2492

Hayden, ID 83835

ISBN-978-0-9838108-0-3

Acknowledgements:

God - You give me strength, vision and passion to make a difference in my life, family and nation; My Hubby Rich - Thank you for your patience, faithfulness and love forever. Nothing worth having is easy; Wayne and Mo - My children. You kids are why our country must remain free and full of opportunity. I love you guys; Steve Eichler - Executive director of Teaparty.org and founder of The Minuteman Project. You are a real friend. Thank you for writing the amazing forward to The people's President; Michael Carlin - Thank you for being the visionary, patriot, professional and dreamer you are. Your belief that I should be President and backing this with publishing my books, your support and creating an amazing Documentary humbles me and blows my mind. Your fearless way of boldly walking forward and trusting God inspires me. www.centurycitynews.com; Sheryl McGrath - My soul sister and best friend. You always inspire, encourage and touch my heart. You are a survivor, leader and best kind of friend. Much love; Phil Berg - Attorney who was one of the first in line to sue Obama on eligibility grounds www.obamacrimes.com. Your courage, ferocity and commitment to the constitution and country are most evident. Thank you for writing the forward for Two Minute Warning, My parents, Neil and Joanne - You always modeled excellence and achievement for me, Think beyond; go further; push through the wall and trust God. Thank you. My brother, Eddie - You are an achieving machine and have kept your heart and life true in the process. I have always admired and loved you; Mary Jensen - My special friend, trusted book keeper and business adviser of 15 years. Your friendship, sacrifice, generosity and patience with me has not gone unnoticed all these years; Joan Swirsky - Thank you for your gutsy truth telling style, friendship and commitment to God and country. You shine in everything. www.joanswirsky.com; Rev. Lainie Dowell - Thank you for your spiritual support, courageous articles, commitment to our Lord and country. You have helped and inspired me in so many areas. www.voiceink.blogspot.com; Phil Berks - My precious buddy from L.A. I met 16 years ago in the music and entertainment business. Thank you for your belief and friendship; Patrick Carey - My trusty call screener and radio show engineer. www.careyengineering.com. Thank you for your amazing faithfulness and quality work. OK, and bad sense of humor; Doug Hagmann - We have broken and covered tons of stories in print and on my show. You are respected and adored by this chick. www. homelandsecurityus.com; ArLeen Lonneker- Friend and Volunteer in the Roth Campaign; Melody and Martin Johnson - My loyal Team from L.A.; Editors of conservative, online journals who have published my articles for years: Judi McCloud – The award winning, principled and brilliant editor of www.canadafreepress.com. You have also been an encouraging and supportive friend for years; Frank Salvato – The Constitution loving editor of www.newmediajournal. us. Your segments on my show each week are awesome; Paul Walters - Courageous editor of www.newswithviews.com and survivor of communism; Jim Kouri of www.conservativebase.com. You have held the courageous light up and broken many stories.

CONTENTS

FOREWORD: *By Steve Eichler*

I FIRST MET DR. LAURIE ROTH on the radio in 2007, as a last
minute guest on her radio talk show. At that point I had been
a guest on more than 1,800 Radio and Television shows over the
course of years, so I was very comfortable with the usual interview
process. However, nothing could have prepared me for the patriotic
passion and genuine political stalwartness Dr. Roth possessed. As
the hour passed, I realized the person at the other end of the phone
was someone far beyond the usual run of the mill talk show host. To
my delight, this patriotic woman was truly and obsessively in love
with America.

Indeed, The Roth Show was Laurie's conduit to America; she was
able to magnify her voice in a manner that few can; not in loudness,
but in content. The more I spoke with her on live radio the more
intrigued I became with the fact she was one of the few female conservative commentators in the media who understood the issues. By
the end of the show I was hoping I would be invited back.

A few days later Laurie called my booking agent and invited me
back to talk about several thorny issues plaguing America. I immediately cleared my schedule ensuring the show took the top spot on my
calendar. Again, her knowledge and political savvy held her audience
spellbound as issue after issue was discussed openly and thoroughly.

I had the opportunity to talk with her off the air and discovered
she is the real deal! From her earned Ph.D. to her Tae Kwan Do black
belt, her motorcycle, her love for her husband and family, her gun
collection and her passion for American exceptionalism identified
her as one of the most interesting people in America, and Lord

knows, I've met a lot of them.

Truthfully, the more I learned about her style of broadcasting current events, the more I realized Laurie Roth was on the right track. One of the problems with America is that so many people are afraid to be themselves, to open up and to speak with honest-to-goodness passion. Too many Americans have been locked into political correctness, unable to escape for fear of being labeled a racist, xenophobe or even worse, a right-wing extremist! So many good-hearted U.S. citizens possess conservative viewpoints, but lack the courage to voice them. For this reason Dr. Laurie Roth is one of a handful of citizens who communicates not just to the people, but for the people, and the people like it!

By 2009 I was a regular guest on The Roth Show discussing issues no one else dared touch. It was then I met other patriots who were forming an upstart political movement named after a historical event in 1773, called the Tea Party. Immediately, I called Laurie Roth, told her about this tiny group and she opened up her show to this thing called the Tea Party. Well, the program was a huge success and she graciously gave one hour per week to the Tea Party calling it, yes, The Tea Party Hour. I believe this was the first nationally syndicated radio talk show to give air time on a consistent basis to the Tea Party. Laurie had the foresight and courage to forge ahead, leading the way for this tiny, fledgling movement that soon surged into a behemoth political power. To this day, The Tea Party Hour is still being heard by millions of her listeners, as a never-ending line of America's "Who's Who" make their appearances on her show. From Dr. Jerome Corsi, the author of over 35 books including Unfit For Command and The Obama Nation. Jim Gilchrist, the co-founder of the Minuteman Project, congressmen, senators, generals and top medical doctors speak fearlessly with Dr. Roth.

At this moment I had no idea what Laurie Roth could do to top her show, but I soon learned her show was just the launching pad for greater things! As I read the original manuscript of this book I was deeply impressed with a sense of her true dedication to God, Country and Family. Laurie's struggle against all odds with her accident, rehabilitation and her comeback is a story astonishing to the average person. Her courage and determination validates how the power of one person with vision cannot only survive, but thrive while inspiring others to greatness.

As the issues are examined and discussed on live radio the audience becomes distinctly aware this moment in America demands a special person able to articulate what American citizens truly believe. They were looking for someone to say it; Dr. Roth is just that person.

I was ever so amazed while reading this book, the one you are about to read, how Laurie addressed issues others are fearful to whisper. Topics we know we believe, but are waiting to hear someone articulate in plain English. Truths we know are foundational to America, which must be stated and then stood upon as a platform are addressed in this book.

I believe every person in America sees without a doubt that "We The People" have our share and then some of problems. We must address these problems with courage and skillfully solve them before the next generation inherits this great country.

Therefore, the problem solvers must be the very people who once looked to Washington for solutions. We have sadly realized our leaders have returned to us empty-handed, confused, disoriented and with no viable solutions. Dr. Laurie Roth is a refreshing voice that calls out to the empty-handed, confused, and disoriented as a beacon of hope with a voice they can hear and a path they can follow and many have.

As you read this book, you will be touched by the true to life story of struggle and triumph. This book is not a bedtime story for children, but a portrayal of a life that will inspire and motivate the reader to reach for greatness.

THE
people's
PRESIDENT

Chapter 1
WHO IS LAURIE ROTH ANYWAY AND WHY DO I CARE?

Why Would Anyone Even Consider Something So Ridiculous As Running For President?

Most of us grow up with dreams or fantasies of what we wanted to be when we grew up. You may recall some of your own wild sounding dreams that Grandma always agreed with. Some of you wanted to be a Movie Star, Famous Singer, Doctor, Lawyer, Astronaut, Mom or Soldier. Some of you even grew up wishing you could be President of the United States some day. You fantasized traveling all over the world in Air Force One, living in the White House and doing things to help your country. It is natural for us all to have dreams and hopes for our future. Some we realize over the years and some we don't.

Of all the fantasies, dreams and hopes I ever had growing up, never once did I imagine, dream or hope to be a politician or end up in the white house. To me the political world I observed on TV and in the news as a kid looked boring, sterile, contrived, kiss up and sound bite theatre, where popularity was the goal and representing real issues was not. They were dressed too formally all the time and had perfect, hair-sprayed hair…those who had hair.

My dream through middle and high school was to be a famous singer and songwriter. I took piano and violin lessons for 10 years and started writing songs in high school. My dream grew and I became very serious about trying to find a record deal. I practiced

1

and practiced and performed everywhere I could think of. Finally, while 19 and in college I saved up and flew to LA to get the 'hoped for Record Deal'. I had no contacts, no money and not even a tape of my music. I was thinking that Capitol Records, MCA and the other big dogs would let me just walk in, sit down at a piano and play my songs. Surely they would see how talented I was and sign me.

After the third record company wouldn't even let me past the front receptionist, nor let me sing for anyone, I dejectedly started walking up and down the streets of Santa Monica, looking at all the used book and clothing stores aimlessly. I was depressed and beating myself up for just wasting what little money I had to fly to LA in the first place. As I moped, trying to figure out what to do next, I noticed a black, Rastafarian, homeless guy lunging at people from one of the alleys as they walked by, roaring like a lion. People would quickly shuffle past him, yell or flip him off. He would do it again and again. I was already depressed but that sight made me even more depressed. What on earth happened to that guy to make him act like that?

I eventually walked down the road to a Safeway and went inside to buy a yogurt and look around. When I walked out I was shocked to see the same guy now sitting on the newspaper stand outside the store. I braced myself and knew what would happen when I walked by him. He would lunge or try and scare me. Sure enough, he jumped off the stand and roared like a lion at me. My adrenaline was flowing but I thought I would do something entirely different so I extended my hand and said, "Hi, I'm Laurie Roth. What is your name?" I'll never forget how he jumped back and said, "You must be very lonely to talk with me." Then he said with dignity his name, that I still remember, but I won't say his last name here for fear of violating his privacy. It was Gregory....

I then invited him to the Burger King at the other end of the parking lot for a burger. He said yes. We were quite the absurd looking couple, me, the nineteen-year old, put-together white girl, and he, the crazy looking, wild haired, crazy acting black guy walking in together for a burger. Yes, we got the looks and mumbles from a few folks.

Our conversation together was interesting and a little strange. At first while he or I would be sharing he would start to laugh incoherently. This happened several times so I finally said, "Gregory, why do you keep giggling and acting insane? Stop it. We are trying to have a little visit here." Shortly after that the incoherent giggling stopped and our conversation got more real and deeper. He revealed over an afternoon of sharing and walking together that he had hitchhiked from Texas to L.A. to find his girlfriend who had left him and gotten into prostitution and drugs. He was robbed and ended up desperate and homeless. As he was treated badly and got more hungry and tired he started acting crazy. The more he acted this way the more people treated him that way and it got worse and worse. We ended up praying together and he said he was planning to hitchhike back to Texas and get his mechanic job back.

After this encounter I felt my spirit lifted and I forgot for a moment about my non-existent record deal. After this I wrote and recorded one of the best songs I ever wrote in my life, "Someone's Waiting for You".

Believe it or not, I had another amazing encounter while in L.A, doing the unexpected and thinking outside the box. I was trying to ride the bus to get to Azusa Pacific University to see a friend of mine, but I had gotten on the wrong bus and was taken to the wrong part of L.A. at dusk, but thought that I was at the right bus stop to connect over to Azusa. I was very wrong. Even the bus driver asked me "Lady, are you sure you want me to drop you off here alone?" I was a little nervous but also embarrassed and trying to act like I had things in control.

So, I got off the bus and looked around. It was nearly dark and then it got worse. I noticed a gang of seven to eight guys hanging out by an alley about half a block from me with chains, knives and other long-looking weapons. Even more horrifyingly they were looking at me and even pointing at me. Now I was in a panic and zero other people were around. I thought quickly of potential options. I knew I couldn't outrun them and had no weapons or help anywhere that I could see. So I quickly said a prayer then decided to do the opposite of what they would expect me to do. I ran to them and said, "Thank God you are here and I found you. What an answer to prayer for me. I was dropped off at the wrong bus stop in this dark and dangerous part of town and didn't know quite what to do. Then I noticed you guys. You are even armed. Would you mind walking me to the right bus stop so I won't be attacked?" What do you think happened then? They did exactly that. They could not have been more warm and helpful. They all escorted me a few blocks to the right bus stop and waved as they put me on the bus. No one touched me or took a thing from me.

When I left L.A. the next day I had no record deal. People didn't hear my music but I saw God work and remind me how important honor and respect were in keeping you alive and how important it is to think outside the box. What a life lesson that was for me.

Years later, I finally did get BMG distribution, sold records around the world, performed concerts and eventually hosted and was one of the producers of a national TV music show called *CD Highway* which aired on over 155 stations on PBS. I interviewed music legends each show like Gino Vannelli, Chicago, Taylor Dayne, Pat Benatar, Chuck Mangione, Rita Coolidge, Blondie, Willy Nelson, Lou Rawls, and Diamond Rio to name a few, as well as new "up and comers." One of the thrilling highlights for me was doing two nationally televised concerts on my show with Rita Coolidge and Gloria Loring. They are fabulous singers and even more fabulous women. The closing theme song every show was The Last Dance, one of the songs I had written and recorded.

After two seasons of *CD Highway* we shut it down. We found it very hard to make enough ad money to survive on PBS due to government restrictions of what advertisers could say in an advert. I was the one pushing, contacting and landing the national advertising to pay our show bills and hopefully raise enough for us to also get paid along the way. It was a major headache finding an advertiser with enough money to advertise on national television that didn't mind reducing their ad down to general talk without "the close."

It was also during the shooting of my TV show that I met and married my "to die for" husband, Rich. I had two broken engagements over the years; obviously I couldn't quite make up my mind, but when I met Rich, it was a hit. That was 11 years ago now. We have two precious children we foster adopted as well, Wayne and Mo.

Though I loved the action of doing a TV show and all the cool interviews, I started missing the live action of radio and digging into hard-hitting issues. I started substituting at a Spokane station that led to an audition at an L.A. station. I got the job and really went to school in "Talk Radio" in that tough market. After a year they sold to a Hispanic network and I was out of a job. However, while there, I grew in confidence and figured out how to finally be myself on air; not contrived, not manipulated "sound bite theatre", not even broadcaster-ish.... Using my heart, humor, wit and passion to entertain, share, discuss the issues and do cutting-edge monologues.

After my year long experience in L.A., I decided to go the next entrepreneurial step and try and go national. I put my budget together, bought broadcast equipment on my credit card (I didn't have any cash), found a couple of advertisers who would take a chance on me, and found a network that would give me a chance if I paid for everything. The attack on our country in 2001 helped focus me even more on talk radio and talk. The country was in shock, ticked off and desperately wanted to talk.

At least, that started my national ball rolling the old fashioned, entrepreneurial way. I would have to do the heavy lifting and ad sales, hosting and prep, but if I did a great job and was relevant I would develop an audience in time. I had a growing vision now to speak my mind on the issues "in our face" as a country. I found a great syndicator that was known for their news and values, IRN: Information Radio Network. I have been with them ten years now and they are wonderful.

I started to be asked to speak at different conferences and was even asked to join a panel with Ann Coulter and Michael Moore on Scarborough Country. Momentum was starting to grow with my brand and show and I was most encouraged and having a blast. I was getting more of an audience on the Internet also, partially due to the following I was receiving from all the articles I regularly wrote on various journals on line. Among these were; www.canadafreepress. com, www.newswithviews.com, www.newmediajournal.us, www. centurycitynews.com, www.arizonafreepress.com, and others who would pick up my articles. After all the years of practically starving I could finally see a bit of growth with my career and show. Then the unbelievable and unthinkable happened. I was nearly killed and it all came to a screeching halt.

Much like America had gone splat on the ground, so did I. My life, career, health, looks, family, spirit, dreams and my finances were crushed and nearly destroyed when I crashed onto the road on my face while riding a motorcycle on August 25, 2005. That day I had ridden to the Mount Spokane Lodge in Washington with my friend, Karen who was also on her bike. It was a hot and beautiful day, perfect for a ride. I wanted to check out a possible date spot for my husband Rich and I for later. Karen and I checked out the restaurant and menu, and rode back down the hill.

I turned a corner at mile marker 14 and found my life's path suddenly and dramatically changed. A deer collided with me and I crashed on my face, nearly breaking everything in my face and slamming my brain against my skull. It gave me severe brain injuries. Was it the end of Laurie Roth?

When Karen noticed my motorcycle hadn't followed her around the corner, she turned back to see me, unconscious, bleeding profusely in the middle of the road and gasping for air. She quickly tried to remove road rash and any broken teeth stuck in my mouth so I could breathe. I wasn't responding to anything Karen tried. She desperately tried to call for help on her cell phone, but it didn't work in the forest where we were. She prayed with all of her heart for a miracle. She wondered if I might die right in front of her.

People started to drive by and to stop, starting with two guys from a construction site down the road who had heard Karen screaming for help. They had miraculously just put in a landline in a few days before. They immediately called for help.

Finally, after 43 minutes the first responders arrived and tried to save me. They knew it was life or death as they saw me bleeding out and gasping for air. They struggled to intubate me, trying to work with the many breaks in my jaw, mandible, the severed roof of my mouth and ripped up gums. My lungs were filling up rapidly with blood and I was dying right in front of them. I was told months later by one of the first responders there that if they had landed and gotten to me even just a few minutes later I would have been dead. They didn't expect me to make it alive to the hospital.

My motorcycle wreck affected almost every area in my life. I learned through nearly a two-year long recovery process, that what I would ever amount to and accomplish again in large part depended on me, my will and desire to choose life, not focus on how things looked or how big "Mount Everest" was in front of me. Did I want to be a well-meaning victim and has-been? Inch my radio show back…or go over the top and create a winning vision of success; physically, emotionally, mentally and spiritually no matter what God had in store for me?

Decisions and seductions to compromise were everywhere along the way. My brain was bombarded more than once with the following visitor: "Laurie, you talk like a stroke victim. You may want to do your national radio show again but even if you get a chance folks will think you are a drunk! Laurie, face it! You have been off the air for ten months. People and radio stations move on. People forget and frankly don't have the energy to care! Laurie, why don't you focus on learning to walk a straight line again and to stop drooling while trying to remember the day you just had."

I learned through my near death experience that God would allow me in large part to chart who I was to become and where I was to go from here. Many would have chosen the wheelchair and settled for the "victim" label. Most medical experts expected that from me…the visitor in my brain wanted that…but my will and life force screamed out for real healing and success, not the obsessive focus on practical reality and circumstances. I started this journey back destitute, physically broken and shredded, yesterday's news, with no health insurance, no energy, looking like Frankenstein and with double vision. Those were just the good parts. I am here to tell you, "THERE IS LIFE AFTER ROAD KILL AND FRANKENSTEIN."

My husband finally had to shut my show down after trying to keep it going for weeks with guest hosts while I lay battered beyond recognition in a hospital bed. He really had no choice since there were also advertising contracts and I couldn't fulfill them. After years of starving, trying to build my independent radio show and finally getting a little progress and audience, bang, it was gone.

Once it entered my head that my national show was gone and just how battered I really was, I started to seek God in prayer and look for ways I could demonstrate love and encouragement to the other patients on my floor. What can I do right now to make a difference as I am tripping to the bathroom? My national scope of influence had just been reduced to a floor of other brain-injured patients.

Most of my time in the hospital during the last few weeks (the only ones I recall) was doing various types of therapy and testing daily.

During mealtime I had an opportunity to visit with other patients. I certainly didn't eat with them because I was only allowed fluid with thickener. Doctors were afraid I would choke and get pneumonia. I remember hearing all kinds of stories of suffering more sad than mine, while I was drinking dinner and they were eating their chicken. It occurred to me more than once that though I didn't understand everything I was going through, I was so thankful for life and a family who loved me! Several of the patients I had talked with had been left and rejected by a lover or spouse in response to a severe aneurysm, stroke or other brain injury. It's not like the movies, people. Not every one can handle suddenly a face and brain that doesn't look or work right!!

I talked with several brain injury patients who looked ripped to shreds like me, but my husband was still coming to see me and theirs weren't. I began to realize how fortunate I really was and how important it was to be thankful for what I had at the moment. It's funny how suffering seems to reduce us all to "the moment", not the future, not the past, not our big plans but "right now." Does that focus on "now" get us anywhere? Well, that depends on what "now" are you focusing on and what "now" are you avoiding or lying about.

Although I remember moments of discouragement and sadness regarding the loss of my show, I remember constantly seeking God to help me get through the day, to do my therapy well and make a difference with someone else. It's not that I was that great of a person, but I did care about people and had been a counselor before all my years in music, radio and TV. I just didn't relate at all to being a victim. I did relate however to achievement and competition. I needed and wanted a challenge to survive past victimhood. What would that be, though? Dreaming about radio and TV again was too abstract and out there! Instead I remember wanting to encourage and help the people in my space. It was obvious the pain and loss surrounding me on that hospital floor was huge. There was a weird sort of comfort knowing in my gut that to the other patients I was just another brain injury patient, not "Dr. Laurie" anything or Talk Show Host! We were all just trying to get through the day somehow while we drooled on each other.

Day after day, I did therapy, more tests and would visit at meal times, then go to bed, just to wake up at 4:00 in the morning again and again. Sleeping patterns were totally messed up. Its amazing that while getting past the grief of losing my face, show, career, dreams and living in the "moment," that focus became two things: Do my daily therapy and exercises the best I could. There were all kinds of daily things physical and mental I was asked to do.

I have to confess I thought I would lose my mind with the endless mental tests: Plan a shopping spree Laurie; find directions on this map Laurie; you have two kids and one needs to get to a piano recital by 3:00p yet you have to get your teenager to basketball practice across town at 4:00p. How do you do that...on and on. I just shut up and did those "mental" exercise tests but I really did wonder if they were trying to give me another brain injury! It felt very patronizing and irrelevant. I felt like screaming at the therapists, I'm brain injured, not mentally retarded! Yes, it's a shock but I haven't lost my ability to think!!

My pride and ego hadn't been totally flattened. Actually, neither had my twisted sense of dark humor. More than once I thought it would be fun to give them what I thought they wanted with the mental story problems. They just knew my sick brain wasn't working and wanted to see that! "Yes, I would leave my four-year old alone at the garage to hitchhike to her recital." What else would a Mom do? "Shopping, huh? I believe in the power of anything colored red so I would only pick up items at the store that were pink or red." "What would I do if my car had a flat tire? Naturally, I would go buy some C4 explosives and blow it up right next to a day care center!" Thankfully I resisted my dark side so I didn't put these types of answers down but I thought about them more than once when rolling my eyes… excuse me, the one that would roll.

The second thing I wanted to focus on in the "moment" was others. I wanted to reach out to others around me and show love. It's ironic and funny how the hyper-focus of these two things, recovery work and focus on others, started to paint a picture of my future right in front of me. God was starting to piece together things way ahead on the trail that I didn't have a clue about.

The day came when I was finally allowed to go home. I was busy packing up my few things when the hospital Chaplain walked in and wanted to talk with me. She shocked my socks off when she told me that I had been an inspiration to everyone who had known me at the hospital including staff and other patients. She went on to tell me how other patients who came to see her had mentioned me again and again. Many talked about how I had encouraged them and listened to them when no one else would.

I remember tearing up and being so touched and thrilled that I was able to offer encouragement to anyone in this situation. I had just wanted to make a little difference while I was in the ⎰

God had just confirmed to my frail ego that I had. The las⌞

had wanted to be while there was "miss fancy talk show host." I hav⌞

always hated airs with people and didn't want to be treated in a special

way just because I did radio. I was Frankenstein who drooled. I just

wanted to help others with strange looking heads and bodies also.

On My Way Home, Now What?

How can I forget the final warning words of my physical thera-
pist, "Don't be alone with your children for awhile; don't drive your
car; and whatever you do don't take your usual walks alone on the
mountain trails." I couldn't help but feel at times that part of the
endless therapy and story problems focused at my brain was to help
stimulate healing…AND…part of the endless therapy and ever so
cautious advice was to protect the doctors from the threat of lawsuit…the big, "in case something happens" and she bashes one of
her kids 'cause she can't take the pressure of parenting now, or she
gets lost in the forest and can't remember her way home. When I left
the hospital I would lie if I didn't admit that I felt the love, the slap
and the fear from many involved. I was a big fat unknown!! What
do we do with Laurie?

A Place Called "Denial"

I knew from my last few weeks in the hospital and my own
background in counseling before music, radio and TV, that many
perceived that I was in denial and not quite getting the severity of
my endless brain and facial injuries. After all, I had asked early on
that the staff take the walker and wheel chair out of my room. This is

after I had been falling and staggering all over the place due to severe inner ear damage. Yes, I will admit it. I sentenced myself early on in the hospital to "Denial" to serve out my time.

I remember the day I was staring at the walker and wheelchair and had made a "denial", but a quality and timely decision. I WOULD NOT BE DISABLED. I WOULD LEARN TO WALK RIGHT AGAIN. NO MATTER WHAT MY CAT SCAN SAID AND DOCTORS SAID!! "Please take the walker and wheelchair out of my room as I won't be falling again." Of course I recognized the ever so sweet and patronizing response from the staff, just waiting for me to fall again to return the wheelchair to my room. We were all ever so polite at this stage.

I am not saying that denial from the reality surrounding you always works to help you, BUT, sometimes, it is just what the Doctor Upstairs ordered! Sometimes it is the path around and through limits, victimhood and the big box you are now in! In my case, I knew the medical limitations and was battered with the doctor's negative opinions. I was the one who had been falling, drooling, talking like a stroke victim and seeing double, remember, so I tasted the medical problems big time! I knew however, that my WILL had to believe enough to ACT IN FAITH that I could walk…WHY…because I WANTED TO and would ACCEPT NO OTHER COURSE! I just made up my mind that I wouldn't fall. Welcome to big "Denial"!!

Where did I get this bizarre notion that I could move beyond my obvious circumstances?? I'll be happy to tell you. I had learned and seen several times before in my life that God honors and actually rewards faith. I found myself recalling the many stories throughout the Bible honoring simple faith, faith to get healing and faith to confront and conquer enemies without the big army and fancy weapons…just belief in God!   Silly little physical limitations didn't intimidate God.

Though some of you may be rolling your practical and cautious eyes about now, allow me to ask you just a small question if I may. How many times do you think I fell in the hospital after I made them take the walker and wheelchair out of my room? (Remember, staggering, tripping and falling was the norm for me.) SHOCK OF ALL SHOCKS!! I NEVER FELL AGAIN IN THE HOSPITAL OR HOME. What could have happened? Did someone lie about my endless brain and balance injuries? Was the CAT Scan a cruel and exaggerated joke? Or, did my will to heal and be well direct and even supercede PHYSICAL REALITY? Did God simply meet me where I laid my little faith and desire on the altar? You tell me.

It's not that I didn't struggle and feel very dizzy many times after that, BUT, I needed the challenge to myself, to the doctors and to the hospital. I made it my "do or die" goal. I would not fall if for no other reason then to have the last laugh in the face of all the patronizing, well meaning and NON-BELIEVING comments I had heard and to the devil I knew wanted to destroy me.   Each day that I had won by not falling, I grew in strength, determination and courage. I couldn't wait to show the world what I could do the next day! Gee, denial is fun and sometimes it is the crazy and God-given path of faith and victory!

I'm Back! Move Over, America And God Haters!

After several surgeries on my mouth I could finally put my lips together correctly and form consonants again. Before my second surgery on the muscles and nerves in my mouth, I talked like a person who had just had ten beers. There was no way I could perform on radio like that. I could just imagine all the liberals who hated me listening and saying, "Listen, Harold, I just knew Laurie was a drunk." I certainly sounded like one.

I practiced every day talking and enunciating words while also exercising my extremely damaged left eye. I kept forcing my eyelid up since it wouldn't open but a little on its own, and forcing light into it. I would also practice looking at a string with little balls placed up and down it, trying to get both eyes to focus on the same ball. The goal was to get my eyes to track together again. This was daily work for two years. I didn't much care to be a remake of the "Columbo" character on TV. At this rate I would be worse if I didn't figure out how to make my left eye come alive somehow.

After ten months of daily therapy, exercise, and practice I was offered my time slot back from my network, Information Radio Network (IRN). I was so excited, but also scared since I was now starting in with just a few stations and had to find sponsors to pay my bills. How could I find sponsors for a national show that was now just three stations in smaller markets? My ego was about as flat as a pancake. I was starting again.

Within a few weeks I found a call screener, Patrick, who wanted to play ball with me, and two sponsors. I started my show again in June, 2006, still recovering from my severe brain injuries and fighting daily exhaustion. At least I was on air again and had my chance. Granted there were only three people and a dog listening but it was a start.

My show was 7-10p PST, my same old time slot but now, by hour three, I was horribly exhausted and with just a handful of stations, I didn't have the caller base I was used to before. I desperately started booking more guests to have someone to talk with on air instead of my constant monologues. There were a few times I was so tired during my third hour that I would fall asleep during my show, then jerk myself back awake hoping no one noticed. I was so not recovered yet but I was now driving a semi down the road.

Unbelievably, I faked my way through and started to feel better slowly as more stations and sponsors came back on. I knew coming back to life and building my show again would be like climbing up Mount Everest in a bikini with no oxygen and I was right. I would look at the news articles all around me and see double vision, barely able to read while fighting endless exhaustion. I kept facing each day as it came with one hand in God's and the other pulling me forward.

My journey back certainly wasn't starring "the pretty girl" because I looked like Frankenstein and drooled for many months. I also had to face this with zero health insurance. Try having nearly a $500,000 accident with no coverage and see if that darkens your day a bit.

I had to trust God because I couldn't see very far in front of me, only enough to take another step and that looked like tilted double vision. Sometimes that is all we have to establish a vision of our best self, throw out our awkward effort that day then do it again tomorrow.

Vision, Prayer, Perseverance And Old Fashioned Work

Now, five years later, 95% of my scars are gone and that is with zero cosmetic surgery. I have been working full time in radio and other projects since 2006, writing and publishing articles weekly for several journals, including www.canadafreepress.com, www.newswithviews.com, www.newmediajournal.us and dreaming big.

Having come so close to death, my dreams and prayers now include more than my career and me, me, me. I am very burdened and concerned for my country. I have prayed for many years, especially since my accident, that God would use me to make a difference and help heal my country.

America has always been a unique and powerful light on a hillside that has supported freedom and achievement. We have stopped the progress and conquests of several evil leaders and movements who planned to take over the world, control and murder people. Let us never forget the sacrifices and bold courage of our military and leaders in WWI, WWII, Korean War, Vietnam War, Gulf War, now Iraq and Afghanistan.

Most of us have noticed for years that America has drifted away from her lead in several key areas. We have shipped more and more of our manufacturing and jobs overseas, drifted further away from our Judeo-Christian values and now watched our freedoms get sucked away in front of our eyes. For the last several decades our tax rates have gone through the roof, back and forth, but mostly up. Then there is our brilliant energy dependence, especially to Islamic dictatorships. What…are we dumb as posts? Maybe you like paying high gas prices. It makes me grumpy and kills my budget.

The world needs us to lead and excel again in business, freedom, hope and opportunity. The only way we will get there and correct our dangerous tilt is to first of all, snap out of our "stupor" and "drift along" mentality and get involved. We must become aware of the bills being pushed and manipulated through congress and start writing, calling and faxing members of the House, Senate and White House. This is our country and they work for us.

The Revolution Is Here, And We Need It To Grow And Continue Through 2012

We have seen a historical and peaceful revolution peppering through our country with the rise of 100 million-plus Tea Party people. No longer is the drift away from freedom and fiscal responsibility acceptable. No longer is it OK to pretend we aren't a Christian nation and drift towards socialism and communism. No longer is it acceptable to hide behind labels seen as powerful: Republican or Democrat. Thanks to the bold and organized efforts of Tea Party groups all across this country we saw the midterms turn dramatically in the Conservatives' direction. It was a major rebuke to the Obama Administration and Democrat Progressives' out of control agenda and assault on common sense, our Constitution, and freedom.

Many of you have asked me to run for President in the 2012 election cycle. I have done what so many of you would do at the suggestion of what seems so impossible, insane and out of touch with reality...laugh and roll my eyes, secretly feeling flattered and wondering.... However, over this last year with the growing pressure placed on me I started to pray about just what I would do to fix and direct my country out of this mess and make her shine again. Ideas started to come to me, and a vision for leadership. Could God Himself be leading something seemingly absurd...putting a REAL person who will listen to Him in the White House?

I wrote this book to share with you my passion motives and specific ideas of what I would do if you voted for someone like me to be "The people's President." I have gotten tired over the years listening to the perfectly timed speeches that say little or nothing about a real and detailed vision to fix our mess. You might wonder and say,

"Laurie Roth has no political experience. What does she know?"

You are right in so many ways and wrong in others. Though not a politician by nature or background, I am currently a local, elected official in Spokane County in Washington State. I started out trying to serve where I live by running for Precinct Committee Officer in my county, then I was elected as Vice Chair of the GOP in my county in which I am currently. County Politics has shown me the horrible distraction of egos, Liberal vs. Conservative agendas, sell-outs and the ability to get stuff done when you focus, work together and try.

I see it the same way on the national and international scene. To deal with all the egos and various agendas in play, we need a President, first who has the character and integrity to serve, who understands human nature, who long ago has placed her ego in God's care and not in the people and Constitution's way. We need a President with an exceptional vision of who America was, is and can become...no, MUST BECOME. That vision must push to have America lead again in manufacturing, business, Judeo-Christian values, freedom, military strength and opportunity. We also need a President with a bold plan to financially free the people and business from exploitive taxation, regulation and litigation so Americans can actually imagine starting a business or inventing something again.

The American way is to vote for what you believe in, who you think can get elected, and who will represent you and the country the best. Each chapter of The people's President will outline specifically what I want to do and will commit to doing if elected. Why do I and others who are pressuring me to run, even think it possible for an outsider, a non-global elitist, Christian, Mom and Non-politician to get elected?

I wouldn't have a chance in any other election until this one in my view. This is largely because you are all organized and committed to stand behind the "real" and "Constitutionally-minded" Conservative this time. Look what the angry and focused people did in the midterms. You must do it again during the Presidential election, break the rules and reflect REAL American values.

Many of you 100 million-plus Americans associate yourself with the Tea Party movement. Thank God for you. I also think it is possible this time because of the dramatic increase in use of the Internet and social networking sites. If things were organized, we had volunteers in all 50 states and there was a strong, viral push on the Internet, we could gain a victory and get busy.

Obama brags already about his billion dollars set aside for the 2012 race. Wouldn't it be something if we could demonstrate that freedom still exists in America and that "we" could get in the White House together and REALLY change things to where they need to be, not shred our Constitution, freedoms, national and international safety and destroy our economy.

I am the one considering the call to run who doesn't have big money. I am the Mom, Survivor and Talk Show Host who speaks her mind and LOVES her country. I am the one whose left eye doesn't work very well anymore and does a national radio talk show with a numb mouth. Listen in at www.therothshow.com.

The only way I could do this and we could win is if you would donate money, organize in your city and state, while helping me to get at least three million signatures to get on the ballot as an Independent. I will go the distance with you if you will go with me. Let us pray that God will put the right person in the White House.

Let me know what you think: www.thepeoplespresident.me

Chapter 2
GIVE US REAL TAX RELIEF

We have heard for years those who have promised tax breaks here and tax breaks there. There is the Fair Tax crowd who has some compelling ideas but still want you to pay a tax of 20-30 percent. That's nice, but doesn't go far enough. Others on the more Progressive left suggest we only give tax reductions of any kind to those earning under $200,000 a year. Those who through the school of sacrifice and hard knocks finally are making $3-500,000 or more, I guess they are to start handing out money to all those around them. It's called "redistribution of wealth" and "punishment for achievement." "You evil people who finally made it, shame on you!!" The more you make the more you should be taxed. That is what the Progressive Left and this President actually believe. That is not only immoral and unfair, but desperately stupid if you want to grow and help your economy. We must run from this notion like the plague.

Remember President Obama didn't even want to keep the Bush tax rate in place. He wanted to increase all our tax levels. Finally through tons of pressure being placed on him he and the Progressive s gave in. Thankfully that was at least extended for two years so we didn't all see a tax increase after the first of the year, 2011, rolled around. Being a Progressive , Redistribution of Wealth Leftist, our President and the Liberals who wrote this made sure there were tons of tax increases peppered all through the "ObamaCare" bill. We saw that home sales were going to be taxed, tanning booths, disability equipment (You evil people with peg legs…pay more, I tell you), less adoption tax credits, cuts on dependent care tax credits, more death taxes, more dividend taxes, forget deductions for tuition and related expenses and make sure investments are taxed. I have just started walking through the sneaky, tax increase pile and I already have a headache. Of course, if Obama's "Health Care Horror" stays in place (God help us) in just a few years I would have to get a prescription from a doctor to even get Excedrin or Tylenol for my headache.

Can you imagine the "criminals" this would create across the country out of sheer desperation? "Tommy, I'll meet you at the corner with my Tylenol shipment. I'll be wearing a long coat and hat. If you pay on time today I'll throw in a box of Excedrin."

Where did this out of income tax get so out of control? It traces all the way back to Karl Marx and his Communist Manifesto where he pushed and campaigned for the idea of redistribution of wealth and taking of income tax from the people. In 1862 to secure support for the Civil War, Congress created the first income tax law. During the 1700 and 1800's all kinds of things were taxed, such as refined sugar, carriages, distilled spirits, tobacco. Shamefully, even slaves were taxed as a product sold. In 1812, we saw gold, silverware, jewelry and watches taxed.

From there it was as if government became drunken cocaine addicts, desperately addicted to the people's money. It made them feel powerful, apparently. Thankfully, Ronald Reagan signed into law the Tax Reform Act of 1986. This was moving dramatically in the right direction. It reduced the top tax rate on individuals from 50-28 percent, but to remain revenue neutral they raised business taxes $120 billion. Then there were the Bush tax cuts that helped some but again were not enough. This whole house of tax cards is an Un-American and unconstitutional way to get money to run bigger and bigger government in my view.

The bottom line is that we lead the free world and have a huge country. Of course government needs money to run. As it stands now, Obama put forth a budget of $3.7 trillion. That is not including the nearly $15 trillion in debt we have. Our government keeps creating more debt while we pay 6 percent in interest each year.

We talk tax increases and tax decreases. One thing in all this is very true. We all pay too many taxes and dread the IRS every April 15th. It is time for a completely new approach that would be a jolt, shock and change for all of us but I am ready for it...are you?

Let's find the quickest way to stop income tax, payroll tax, capital gains tax, gas tax, ALL taxes except for a point of purchase, national sales tax of 2 percent to run the country and pay down our debt. CPAs, tax and money experts have told me that there is at least $400-500 trillion in government transactions each year that could be taxed, including the stock market and Wall Street. If we didn't waste all kinds of money and time on exemptions we would have more than enough to get quickly out of debt and pay all our bills.

I talked with an attorney recently and asked how to proceed on something like this, if President. You would simply have to have a bill presented to congress for a vote. It would not have to involve any constitutional challenge or change. It is simple if we just had a leader with the will to do it and who will stop stealing from business and individuals! Let's get this Tax Bill signed into law and stop all the other taxes accept perhaps tariffs placed on products coming into the US from other countries.

Assuming the 2 percent tax on at least $400 trillion in government transactions, you would have $8 trillion each year to work with.

Lets look at what could be done with it.

Assuming Obama's own budget of $3.7 trillion before review and cutting of waste and duplication, you could still do some needed and awesome things for the country, while paying $3-4 trillion each year to chunk down the debt. Think of it. Our debt would be down to zero in 4-6 years and the value of our dollar would soar internationally.

Transitioning to a 2 percent national sales tax would act as a financial revolution, healing our country of her out of control debt, giving money back to individuals and businesses again and allowing enough in our national budget each year to address real concerns and priorities. Among these would be Social Security, Medicaid, Medicare/CHIP and our Military. It would also allow us to do a shotgun plan to create energy independence. Unless of course you like being dependent on the Middle East for oil and paying $50 to fill up your gas tank.

Why have our Republican and Democrat Presidents up until now not tried this? I asked an elected official why he thought no one had done this and he said that politicians in power don't want to give up the control on the people. They like the power of controlling people and their money so they wouldn't possibly want to stop taking income or payroll tax. How attractive. Now can I throw up?

The irony in all this is that if you had a point of purchase 2% tax on everything, no exemptions, your taxing pool would be so much that you would at least bring in $8 trillion a year, you could do all you needed to and wanted to, while chunking down your debt. This taxation could all be done by freeing both the people and business. How is that anything but right?

If you put me in the White House, this will be one of the very first things I do with you, change to a national 2 percent sales tax and stop dead in their tracks all the other taxes to the American people.

Chapter 3
ENERGY INDEPENDENCE

Let's Start With Oil

Here is the full meal deal. We need and use a ton of energy. According to Texas oilman and natural gas expert, T Boone Pickens, America uses 25 percent of the oil produced throughout the world and we have 4 percent of the population. We import over 68 percent of the oil in this country and from mostly people who hate our guts.

So, what do we have here? We import most our oil and get it from people who don't like us, use too much compared to the population we have and aren't getting any closer to energy independence while the Middle East burns up and becomes more unstable. That just gives me a whole lot of warm fuzzies inside. Perhaps we should just line up and shoot ourselves in the head.

To add to our oil dependency and addiction, we have environmentalists who are also off the "dumber than a post" meter. The essence of their concern is awesome in that we must protect the environment we live in, but long ago they established the impossible rules…their way or the highway.

Environmentalists these days would rather bankrupt ranchers and food producers up and down California than to possibly risk smelt (fish) getting stuck in a water pipe. Naturally, with the huge danger of a 1-2 inch fish getting lost in a water pipe, officials shut off the water to some of the most productive and rich farmlands in the country. That was really using their heads; helping to ruin

California's near-destroyed economy. This is the typical, off the scale response of the radical environmentalists.

Fish are nice, but people, ranches and jobs are nicer. I can't help but notice over the years there is rarely common sense when discussing the environment. All REAL considerations need to be involved; animals, environment, corporations AND people. You know...those pesky things...PEOPLE, we hear about sometimes in the movies?

I love animals and nature like a good chunk of Americans. In fact, I am a dog-owning, animal freak who has rescued tons of animals and feeds deer, raccoons and flying squirrels at my feeders every day. I don't want corporate, greedy thugs to kill animals and destroy nature. The two dogs I have now are rescues. They are big babies and sleep on my couches and beds. "Dog Hair Central"...that is the name of my estate.

We need to solve our energy problems. What we have desperately needed for years is sane debate and conversation where we can develop the energy sources we need to achieve energy independence AND care for our environment and animals. We can do it all if politics, egos, communist ideologies and morons get out of the way.

Regarding Oil

We use roughly 20 million barrels of oil per day and we only produce 5.1 million barrels of oil a day. 45 percent of all this is used for motor gasoline and the rest for jet fuel and other oil usage. Up until 1970 we produced enough oil on our own to supply our demand in the U.S., then we started importing oil after that. In 2007, the U.S. imported from 46 different countries.

The top five countries we import from are; Canada, 18.61 percent, Saudi Arabia, 14.50 percent, Mexico, 14.07 percent, Venezuela, 11.48 percent and Nigeria, 10.80 percent. Smaller importers of oil to the U.S. include; Angola, Iraq, Algeria, Ecuador and Kuwait. This translates to OPEC countries making up 53.85 percent of all U.S. oil imports.

In case you hadn't noticed, the Middle East is not exactly stable, and these days, is in upheaval. Maybe we should just stop drilling what we do drill and get all our oil from OPEC. Maybe we should approach Iran for oil since we are on a "stuck on stupid" roll.

While educating myself about the oil industry, I discovered with all this demand and dependence on foreign oil, we haven't built any refineries since 1976. Many have blamed this lack of forward momentum and drilling on too many environmental regulations and expenses but that would be just part of the "fuel and oil stoppage" story. There are also government subsidies that have been offered for smaller refineries that aren't running as efficiently as the larger refineries. Our government offered extra rights and money to these smaller refineries from 1973-1980. When all these handouts stopped, you guessed it: Many refineries went under. It's funny how so many people and companies in our country get addicted to handouts, then when they finally stop and they are expected to take the ball and run, they crash and burn. Then they go on Oprah, get an attorney and sue someone for damages.

In 1976 we went from 18.6 million barrels of oil a day to 16.8 million barrels of oil a day. Back in 1981 we had 325 oil refineries and now 149. Many of these went under because they were inefficient while others were dependent on government price control programs that finally stopped. Some were inefficient and dependent on government handouts.

Oil Reserves

According to the EIA, the U.S. has a reserve supply to last us about three and a half years without importing oil from elsewhere. We use 6.6 billion barrels per year and have on hand 21 billion barrels. That at least gives us a cushion.

The bottom line of all this is that we use and need more oil than we create and we get over 50% of our oil from OPEC countries. That is beyond stupid and a national security risk in my view. We should be doing research and expanding key oil refineries we have while developing and creating new ones.

What Is The Problem?

We have too many regulations that stop and stall drilling and development. In addition, finding up-front money to build refineries is a problem. I believe our government should help with grants. It is estimated each refinery will cost between $4-6 billion. With all the money this government has wasted on nonsense, studying condom use with prostitutes in China, and mice in the Bay Area, you would think putting money into energy independence would be money well spent.

Assuming the country is bringing in $8 trillion from a 2 percent national sales tax, (no other tax – see my plan in Chapter 2) we should set aside $300 billion to do a shotgun approach to creating all kinds of energy. We could give grants to build new oil refineries and expand current refineries. For a grant of up to $6 billion, to build an oil refinery, the deal should be as follows: The oil refinery agrees to give 75 percent of their oil to the U.S. first, then sell to the world market the last 25 percent. Of the 25 percent in world market sales, I think it is fair to pay the U.S. Government 5 percent of those sales to then be sent out equally to the American people in a yearly check.

When I mention that government should supply billions of dollars in grants to build oil refineries, I am not talking about buying or controlling them as Obama has done with the auto industry. The only control I think is appropriate for extending a 4-6 billion-dollar oil grant is to require that the energy is placed in the U.S. first and that they give a 5 percent payment on foreign sales to the American people.

If we got started in 2012, within three-four years we could have many expanded oil refineries and several new refineries, moving dramatically to increase the oil we create instead of importing so much.

We should set aside $50 billion for the creation and expansion of oil refineries. That would be enough to update and expand what we have, while building more key oil refineries in places of promise.

Nuclear Energy

You may not have known this, but we have 104 nuclear power reactors in 31 states. These are operated by 30 different power plants. In 1980, these plants produced 251 billion kWh, which is 11 percent of the U.S. electricity we use. In 2008, the output had increased to 809 billion kWh and 20 percent of electricity, and 30 percent worldwide. According to www.world-nuclear.org/info/inf41.html, this increase came from 47 reactors, all approved and coming on line in the 1970s and 1982. This more than doubled our U.S. nuclear generation capacity.

A lot of us are stuck in the fear zone even at the thought of developing or building nuclear plants since the highly publicized Three Mile Island accident in 1979 and Chernobyl in 1996. There was the 1985 Mexico City 8.7 earthquake that killed over 10,000 people, and in 2011, the Japan nightmare 9.0 monster that also killed upwards of 25,000 people and compromised their nuclear reactors.

However, even with this industry fighting uphill with all the media distortion and fear cards real and imagined, they have achieved huge gains in safety systems, maintenance and improved refueling strategies. The truth is, any mega-earthquake hitting any energy system, oil refinery, natural gas plant or nuclear plant would cause catastrophic leaks, breakage and damage. We need oil, natural gas and nuclear power. The world must have energy but can't control nature and its fury. Sometimes lightning strikes and causes catastrophic forest fires. Sometimes tornadoes destroy homes and cities, while killer hurricanes level and destroy coastlines and islands. Earthquakes also have a mind of their own and no matter how cautiously we watch them and try and avoid fault lines, they still destroy. The only option we have is to try to create as many safety plans and systems with all energy facilities.

It is time in our country to make sure all 104 nuclear reactors are running with the highest safety standards and producing all they can for American energy needs first. We should set a total of 50 billion dollars of the $8 trillion coming in annually, for nuclear upgrading, new building and development. Let's go for increasing nuclear energy capability from 20-40 percent of our nation's energy. We should lead by having the most upgraded and safest nuclear facilities on earth.

Coal

Coal has been our mainstay and one of our largest energy providers since the beginning of this country. One quarter of the world's coal reserves are located in the United States. According to the U.S. Department of Energy, the energy content of the nation's coal resources exceeds that of all the world's known recoverable oil. It is also the main provider of our nation's electric power industry. It provides more than half the electricity consumed by Americans.

We have too much coal, too much history with coal and too much need for energy to lower our production of coal and to make it harder for this industry. However, we have a President who made one of his energy crushing goals most clear when running for President: "I haven't been some coal booster." and "If they want to build a coal power plant, they can, but it will bankrupt them." These statements are extraordinarily misguided. Mike Carey, president of the Ohio Coal Association, had a response: "Regardless of the timing or method of the release of these remarks, the message from the Democratic candidate for President could not be clearer: the Obama-Biden ticket spells disaster for America's coal industry and the tens of thousands of Americans who work in it."

Obama talked during his campaign of wanting to bankrupt the coal industry, but couldn't wait until we all paid four-five dollars a gallon. Remember that one? Well, from the look at the pumps last week when I was taking my kids to school, he is fulfilling his dream. Americans are suffering and paying four-five dollars a gallon. Obama must be in ecstasy. Where did Obama get his energy policy? He says we can't drill for oil, yet he gives Brazil $2 billion to drill for oil. He wants to bankrupt coal but he is most happy to build windmills. You know, with all the gas and wind power coming from the White House, perhaps we should check for radiation leaks there. Obviously this President has no energy policy nor will to bring down energy prices. As President, I would recommend giving this amazing industry $25 billion in grants to continue to grow, build and increase safety and cleanliness standards.

Let's move on to another outstanding source of energy that must be developed.

Natural Gas

Natural gas is the next big wave of our energy future. It is 50 percent cleaner than diesel and gasoline. Right now there are ten million vehicles in the world that run on natural gas. There are only 142,000 using natural gas in the U.S. Right now we lack infrastructure and natural gas pumping stations to fuel our cars. With the right leadership in the White House we could get this done and bring independence and sane prices to our doorstep.

Iran has changed to using natural gas as their key source of energy because they have a ton of it and it is cheaper and cleaner. Why aren't we? We have the biggest supply in the world right here. Oh yeah, we can't because this President doesn't want our energy more affordable for us and independent.

T Boone Pickens, oil and natural gas mogul who took Mesa Petroleum to be the largest independent oil producer in the U.S., has a whole ton to say about the importance of our country utilizing natural gas and getting independent. He has put his money where his mouth is, as well. He spent over $60 million to promote alternative sources of energy. His message: Natural gas must replace petroleum.

"It's cleaner, it's cheaper, it's abundant and it's ours."

I don't know about you, but I'm sold. 50 percent cleaner, we have a ton of it and it is significantly cheaper. Where is our wallet? Let's see, our energy budget was $300 billion. We have set aside $50 billion for oil development and improvements, $50 billion for nuclear upgrades and improvements…I say we spend $75 billion for natural gas infrastructure and creation. Let's put the natural gas pumps everywhere and get most of our cars running on it.

We know we can expand, clean up, develop and grow oil, nuclear and the big one, natural gas, but what about other not-so-publicized ways to help our energy situation?

Solar Power

Solar technology has jumped dramatically forward. Solar panels have increased their efficiency by 300 percent in the last few years with magnifying film technology. There are more and more companies buying property and putting up enough solar panels to create much needed power. In Southern Colorado there is a 19 megawatt solar power plant. The Greater Sandhill Solar plant in Alamosa County, Colorado, is supplying annual electricity for 6,700 homes. There are numerous and growing solar plants all over the country.

The bottom line is that solar power is renewable, clean and is a common sense solution in Sun Belt states and areas. Individuals and businesses can save huge on this. Think of what you could do as a family or business if you had an extra $400-1000 a month saved from utilities?

Back to our pot of 2 percent tax money for energy: I would suggest we set aside $25 billion to offer grants to build many new solar plants and to fuel more research in this area. Since this technology is advancing forward and could be used to save people money in many parts of the country, I would offer a one-time grant of up to $20,000 to a person 21 and older to get set up with solar panels.

Algae Fuel

Algae is a little gem we are going to hear more and more about. It is an alternative to fossil fuel and comes from natural deposits. There are already many companies and some government agencies funding and pushing to move this along and make fuel production viable. Though algae costs more per unit, it yields between 10-100 times more energy per unit than oil. Some in the industry say it like this: The United States Department of Energy estimates that if algae fuel replaced all the petroleum fuel in the United States, it would only require 15,000 square miles, which is only 0.42% of the U.S. map. Algal Biomass Organization Head, Mary Rosenthal said, "We're hoping to be at parity with fossil fuel-based petroleum in the year 2017 or 2018...." They are demanding production tax credits. I have a better idea. How about offering the Algae World grants for development and research to the tune of 25 billion?

One of the key and critical goals of the next President and Administration must be to get America on the fast track to energy independence for the sake of our economic health, meeting our growing energy needs and national security. If we do this right and get oil, nuclear, natural gas, coal, solar, algae, all growing, building, producing and doing it safely, we can create a huge income stream for our country. We can do this by exporting what we don't need and use.

Energy independence and development must be one of the major goals of the next administration. There is no reason for us to import any energy and every reason for us to develop enough to be able to export energy, even after we use what we need and create.

Think $300 billion in development and energy independence grants. This is out of our $8 trillion coming in from our 2 percent tax:

$75 billion – oil

$75 billion – nuclear

$75 billion – natural gas

$25 billion – solar

$25 billion – algae/alternative fuels

First, you have to get the right President in the White House who carries this vision and the vision of the people. We can do this if you will help me. www.thepeoplespresident.me

Chapter 4
STANCE WITH OTHER COUNTRIES

Regardless of whom we are dealing with, we must be a shining light on a hill, reflecting freedom and worth for people. Our Constitution and Bill of Rights should guide us in ways that show courage but also wisdom. Just because governments aren't democratic or don't agree with us doesn't mean we automatically look for conflict and potential war. However, we must decide what our real goals and general position will be in the world that is consistent and moral. There is evil. There are uprisings, and there is danger we must respond to.

What About How We Have Handled Libya?

In March 2011, The United Nations Security Council authorized international action to keep Libyan leader Moammar Gadhafi from slaughtering the freedom fighters. We were told that the outgunned rebels were in retreat and the U.N. backed any measures to protect civilians there.

At first I found it most interesting that the French and British quickly rallied for an attack. Then I found that Libya was their main oil provider. The U.S. gets no oil from Libya. Now what? How should we be thinking of this "new" war thrown upon us? There was no discussion or approval from congress. There were no official warnings and resolutions from the U.N. demanding certain actions from Gadhafi or an attack would be imminent. The U.N. Security Council authorizes "all necessary measures" and "broke new ground in backing international action to protect civilians" (Reuters, May 13,

2011). That wasn't clear and good enough in my view. There needed to be specific resolutions from the U.N. as there was with Saddam Hussein, demanding specific behavior changes and dialogue by a certain time or else he would be attacked.

There was no declaration of war, nor was there any threat of attack or attack on the U.S. The heart of the problem seems to be a civil war and unrest within the country. No one wants to see civilians murdered in any country. However, countries are also sovereign and dictatorships are plentiful worldwide. Where do we go next to stop murders and abuse…Iran, North Korea, and Palestine?

With this approach to Libya, there seems to be little agreement or plan among the allies, no support from Congress or the American people and frankly no assurance that spending hundreds of millions in missile attacks will accomplish anything to help the freedom fighters and civilians. In my view, this is not the smart move for us in Libya. There should have been bold and quick leadership by our President given against Gaddafi's actions, pushing for a clear and bold U.N. resolution stating the required actions and swift consequences. That would have accomplished a whole lot more for peace and getting the right action from this thug than lobbing hundreds of U.S. missiles into Libya without a real plan.

What Stands Should America make? Islam and Sharia Law

There are numerous things America must boldly stand against in many ways using Twitter, Facebook, other social networking sites, the Internet and freedom supporting shows on Satellite TV peppered through dangerous and abusive areas. One of the ongoing horror shows of abuse throughout the Muslim world involves the daily abuse of women and denial of basic rights. Where are the women's groups? Where is the ACLU? Where is NOW? Where is Hillary Clinton on this? They are all AWOL. America needs to grow a backbone and lead on this, not create wars, but make bold stands against the use of strict Sharia law in any Muslim country; where gays are executed, rape victims are whipped, those converting to another faith are executed, wives are beaten and have no real defense, and hands are cut off. This cannot stand.

We can't declare war on the entire Muslim world, nor should we, but we can do a lot better about standing for human rights. Regardless of the religion people ascribe to, massive beatings, abuse, and denial of rights for people of difference and women cannot be tolerated if we are to do business and have any close associations with them. This is yet another reason why America must pursue a fast track to energy independence so we can make more objective, sound and moral decisions with other countries.

Themes That Must Not Be Ignored By America

We can't let governments commit genocide and just mow down people who stand for freedom or are simply a minority. We must stand behind governments where we can and draw them toward democracy and freedom, however, we must know that not all governments and leadership will be drawn to freedom.

We made a big mistake with how we handled the Green party in Iran back in 2009. The Greens rallied the people, were marching in the streets, and desperately seeking America's help and support. They believed that elections were rigged by Mahmoud Ahmadinejad, and thousands were standing against him. They were no doubt right. Where were we?

Because Ahmadinejad was arresting and murdering civilians everywhere, and because he was a long-term enemy to America and to Israel, our ally, let alone pursuing nuclear aspirations, we should have boldly stood behind the Green party and protestors. We should have used Twitter and Facebook campaigns, satellite TV and messaging, and sent in stealth military operatives to support the uprising and stop the murders. In my opinion, if we had done that instead of desperately distant, mild rebukes that meant nothing, Ahmadinejad would have been out by now and pro-Western leadership would have been in place, thus helping to stabilize the wildly inflammable Middle East.

In 2011, we have seen uprisings all over the Middle East where countless thousands have been standing against oppressive regimes. From Tunisia, to Egypt, Jordan, Libya, Saudi Arabia, and more, the Middle East is on fire in many ways and calls for our response. What will it be?

We hear that Obama is supporting civilians and defending people from slaughter. If Obama were concerned about the health and welfare of freedom fighters and civilians, he would have done something real to intervene and stop the murders and massive arrests against the Green movement in Iran in 2009.   He did nothing but speak a distant and quiet rebuke. If Obama cared about human rights, he wouldn't have given Hamas, an Islamic terrorist group with a history of attacking Israel, $900 billion. If Obama were so concerned about freedom fighters in Libya, he would have opened his silent mouth regarding the suffering and oppression around Costa Rica, when Calero Island was viciously occupied by the Sandinistas last

November. There was no Obama crying, talking or praying for them.

It All Comes Back to American Independence and Energy

We have heard speech after speech from Obama and his Leftist Administration how he is not for us drilling for oil, environmental this, and money that. In fact, after the BP spill, the oil well of independence and drilling for America was poisoned even further. Yet, interestingly, Obama has been kissing up to Brazil and has given them $2 billion to drill for oil. The kicker here that is beyond insanity are his recent comments where he said he wants to help develop Brazil's offshore resources so America can one day import its oil from them. Have I lost my entire mind?

Obama's lack of leadership and continued damage to America is impeachable. Just think what $2 billion could have done to either expand 2-3 refineries making oil for America or have a brand new refinery half built.

Real leadership in the White House would make it front and center to build energy independence, developing all the energy we have; oil, nuclear, natural gas, solar and alternative fuels. This should have been accomplished decades ago. I can't blame it all on Obama.

Our energy plans and plants should be built, updated, enhanced for safety and efficiency, WHILE attending to the environment and animals! I don't want any more bridges to nowhere and studies of condom use in African males. I want energy independence and cheap fuel for my car!

My prediction is that if we spent $2-300,000 billion to do just that and develop ALL our energy facilities, we would create 100 percent of the energy we need and more so. We would be exporting our extra energy and be making a ton of extra money for the country while our gas prices would go down.

Radical socialists, global elites and pretend Americans, be gone. It is time for real leadership, energy independence, real tax reform and compassionate leadership in the world. Make 2012 count. If we can't get off the globalist and socialist stupid machine, one of us might have to run to get things in order. We have seen what the politicians and self appointed messiahs do. Maybe a Mom, Survivor and Talk Show Host might do better. (www.thepeoplespresident.me)

I am certainly not against seeking out allied and U.N. support regarding international skirmishes and genocide, but America must do the right thing in defending life regardless of what other countries or the U.N. says. We can't respond because of oil concerns, economic plays and intimidation to Islam.

We must find technological ways to support freedom in the Middle East and throughout the world. We should be using Twitter, Facebook, social networking sites and pro-West satellite TV programs, which promote western values and freedom. More and more groups will have the courage to stand up for freedom and their rights if they know the West will rally behind them and they won't be left to die.

Remember Rwanda?

Another genocide that occurred, fell during the Clinton administration when Rwanda saw nearly 1 million Tutsis slaughtered by the Hutus in 1994. When Bill Clinton finally sent nearly 1,000 troops in, the murders instantly stopped and order happened. He did this way late in the genocide. I can't help but wonder that if we had responded quickly with even 500 troops, maybe 2/3 of the people would be still alive. Instead, our government did nothing until much too late. What good is talk and more talk when murders are happening? This whole drama was VERY different than Libya. It was an out of control slaughter. I know, I had one of the Tutsi survivors in my home for months during that time.

There will always be uprisings through out the world. America must deepen our relationships with our allies and cultivate other allies and friends, while standing in every way possible for freedom and human rights. I believe we should take the proactive step in advance, throughout the Middle East and oppressive regimes, to use Twitter, networking sites, Facebook and freedom-promoting satellite TV programs.

We must get people everywhere the real message of the West, and freedom. That should help to rise up people in oppressive regimes to stand against and overcome tyrants. We should support them in every creative and innovative way possible. When absolutely necessary to stop slaughter, we should use surgical strikes quickly and get out.

What About China And Trade?

China and the U.S. are the two largest economies in the world. We go back a long way in dealing with Communist China. Each administration is slightly different on the issues between the two countries. Three of the main ongoing issues involve Taiwan, trade and human rights. China has always viewed Taiwan as their 23rd province and even threatened to take it by force. That pressure builds with Taiwan wanting to declare independence and China wanting to push for ownership. The bottom line over several administrations is governed by the Taiwan Relations Act, that has stated a commitment to a One China policy, but doesn't say if the U.S. actually agrees with the position.

It seems we are all in a status quo kind of flow game to avoid a big conflict. The Taiwan people also share a general public consensus for keeping things as status quo. The U.S. has tended to back off from supporters who want to declare independence in Taiwan, since that brings bigger threats to swoop in from China. I think it is critical to continue support for Taiwan and continue to increase the health and honesty of our relationship with China. Status quo seems to be working with this issue.

America must also court, inspire, promote and campaign for more human rights and freedom in China. We must do this by keeping communication open, drawing lines in the sand where there are real consequences for human rights abuses, and putting pressure on China economically and with tariffs where need be.

Regardless of China's choices to grow in freedom, we must pay off our debts as quickly as possible to China and pursue fair trade, where we both win not just China.

What About Israel?

America has always been a long-standing close friend and ally with Israel. However, that friendship and common sense support has been compromised many times and throughout several administrations.

I am all for great dialogue and negotiations that make sense with Arab neighbors, but the push over the years for Israel to give back land and give away land is wrong. They have been attacked almost nonstop since 1948 by their Muslim neighbors and in every war they have cleaned clock and beat their adversaries. Yet, over the last several decades we have heard droves of complaints, whining, direct and indirect attacks demanding land be returned to surrounding Muslim countries. They want the land back that Israel rightfully took in war put upon her that she didn't even start.

Israel has been open to a Palestinian, two state solution from day one back to 1948, but the Arab/Muslim world was not, end of story. With all the distorted talk over the years about a two state solution with Palestine, they have never once done the first and common sense step to create peace by putting into their constitution and announcing to the press and Muslim world that Israel even has a right to be a country next to them.

What has been the point of all the "peace" negotiations when Palestinian leadership from way back, won't start by stating that Israel has the right to exist there? There is nothing to talk about until Palestine changes that policy and stops supporting Islamic jihadists and suicide bombers attacking Israel. Once Palestine makes a real and tangible step of changing their constitution to allow Israel to exist and announcing this change to the entire world, then it is time for discussions on a two state solution and that cannot include more land and territory giveaways by Israel.

I was horrified when Obama gave the Muslim radical and terrorist leadership, Hamas $900 million after none of the above compromises and regular attacks and support of attacks for many years against Israel. That was no way to support our best ally in the Middle East and in the cause of freedom. That was, however, Obama's usual way of kissing up to radical Islam.

Strength, Wisdom, Loyalty and Morality

Regardless as to who the U.S. is dealing with; Russia, China, the Middle East, Europe, North Korea, disasters abroad, we must first have a clear idea as to who we are and defend our Constitution, law and Judeo-Christian values. We must respect difference, even awkward difference, yet assertively promote in every way possible human rights, freedom and opportunity. Wars and violence are the very last solution.

Common sense to me says we stand for Israel in consistent and loyal ways, stand against radical Islam and the abuse toward differences and women in Sharia law throughout Islam. We must strengthen our communication and bonds with China and Russia, but stand boldly for human rights changes, growth and fair trade.

Finally, I am all for healthy international relationships if we first protect our security, way of life and values. I am not for international treaties, such as the START treaty Obama signed with Russia. There have been all kinds of pushes for treaties, including the Rights of a Child treaty through the U.N. that Hillary wants. There continues also to be the push for a U.N. controlled international court.

All of the treaties listed above violate our sovereignty and security in my view. Regarding our nuclear strike capability, Ronald Reagan built up our nuclear capacity for a reason. It is a strong deterrent against evil. It was a great mutual deterrent with Russia for years and should continue to be so for any evil regime that wants to attack the U.S. with weapons of mass destruction. It is stupid in my view to limit these and pretend as if there will be real accountability and proof of these mutual limitations with Russia. There would be nothing but double books and lies probably from all parties involved. It doesn't take rocket science to figure that out. Let's undo the START treaty and stop this naive nonsense.

The Rights of a Child treaty has wanted to give so many rights to kids that spanking would be a reported crime and possibly get a CPS worker visiting your home. If you were a Christian family who went to church on Sundays and your rebellious 13 year-old girl decided she didn't want to go but you made her, she would have an official right to a complaint. She could even be taken from your home. The bottom line of all this Rights of a Child nonsense, is it is U.N. control over family systems in America and wherever they can get their hands on. No one with a brain wants to abuse and beat their children, but I don't know of any parents who have not had to spank their child for something. This would make parents criminals for just being parents and existing. Apparently, Hillary has grown in her world view from "It Takes a Village" to raise a kid to "It Takes the U.N. to raise a kid." No, thank you.

Finally, there has been a push for years to get the U.S. to rally behind a U.N. controlled International Court to settle abuse, war crimes and other crimes in various countries. My problem with that is that the U.N. is not trustworthy and has so many Muslim controls that I would be most concerned as to how they even defined crimes and who would be in charge of pursuing justice. Would it be a tad bit of Sharia law, global elite/sovereignty-violating justice, Israel-hating revenge justice, One World religion and 50-yard-line justice? Yes, yes and yes. No thank you.

We need to come up with a concept of REAL objective, international justice that is not adjudicated by an Islamic, Sharia agenda, environmental global warming agenda, One World religion agenda or international redistribution of wealth agenda.

Chapter 5
LET'S TALK FREEDOM AND HUMAN RIGHTS

Our freedom, worth and uniqueness comes as a gift from the God of the Holy Bible. It is not granted to us by government, religious traditions, loaned to us when we are in thick with the current leadership or the right sex or race. Get it? It is a gift. That is where we all are meant to start our life dialogue.

Freedom comes from God. He has told us for thousands of years about our worth and value in story after story in the Old and New Testament of the Holy Bible. It was that inspiration that fired up rare courage, sacrifice and determination to move to a foreign land, and stand as the small, "sheep smelling" David (America) stood against the "huge and powerful" Goliath (British Government) and win against all odds.

We saw our country sacrifice blood, lives, and money to protect and keep freedom against evil tyrants and agendas in war after war. From the Nazis to the Communist regimes and now the Islamic radicals, we stand. That is the American way and in case you didn't notice, freedom is not free and rarely found in the world.

How Does Freedom Get Chipped Away?

Sadly it is one of the elements of human nature to try and dominate and control one another. We see the "stronger consume the weaker." It is a story again and again that plays around the world, the big, powerful, evil money people who take over the scared and submissive worker bees.

The story is almost boring by now. The evil tyrant fantasizes his kingdom of power and fame. He then manipulates the struggling economy, health and security concerns of the people. He appears for a time as "Father Christmas", the "savior of change and hope" and the "deliverer." Naturally, as the tyrant manipulates the trust of the tired and desperate people, he creates enemies elsewhere that are imagined. Once the dictator has gained power, the oppressive wagons of his evil arrogance start to circle the people. He now loans out freedom as he defines it and controls the people.

The gifts, rewards and money go out to very few in the tyrant's realm of power. The struggling worker bees get handed dog bones as they become more oppressed by rules and laws. Many are killed, thrown in prison or arrested if they don't comply. Meanwhile, the imagined enemy continues to be attacked while other enemies are created as needed.

Just a few of the many dictators who wiped out millions, after they were put in by the trusted and naive people include:

Yakubu Gowon of Nigeria - 1.1 million deaths
Mengistu Haile Mariam of Ethiopia - Led a communist militia and led 1.5 million to their deaths

Kim Il Sung of North Korea - Brought 1.6 million to their deaths

Pol Pot of Cambodia - In his desire to cleanse the country he murdered 1.7 million people

There are so many it would take a whole book just to outline the many blood-crazed, power addicted murderers who have ruled. I will skip past many and go to the last three you may recall, as follows:

Adolf Hitler, the Nazi party dictator of Germany - Was responsible for 17 million deaths.

Jozef Stalin, first Secretary of the Communist Party - Wiped out 23-50 million people.

Mao Zedong - Communist leader of China who murdered 49-78 million people

The sobering truth about all of these dictators was they appeared at first like the savior of hope for the poor and middle class. They were bringing jobs, food, security and health care. Lies, lies and more lies.

Freedom is one of the essential ingredients for happiness in life. It has been one of the rare ingredients that made America the leader of the free world. It is impossible to think outside the box, create solutions, invent amazing things and business when you are strictly controlled and any financial reward for success is taken and redistributed. Freedom is a God-shaped void in all of us and well worth fighting for.

We Must Lead in Peace and Stand Against Evil

Obama golfs, and picks NCAA favorites while the Middle East melts down.

How do we even begin to describe the leadership style and behavior of President Obama? Just some of the many things that come to mind as he has responded to the building Middle East crises, especially Libya, are his U.N. empathetic passivity and total lack of courage and leadership in protecting civil rights. He displays a total lack of competency and ability to lead the free world to stand for those begging for America's help and intervention. He is a bold failure.

Up until this lame administration, it was a given that we would lead, confront and take out those who were evil and killing others. The world actually counted on us to be the "good guys" and act. We used to stand no matter what the tilted, highly Muslim-influenced U.N. would say. We pursued what was right.

Now we hear Obama and Hillary saying America won't go first and lead in our response to Libyan leader Moammar Gadhafi wiping out thousands of his people who dare to march in the streets, picket and stand for freedom. In Gadhafi's world, either the people love and obey him to the letter or they will die.

Events and murders were happening all over Libya for 10 days before we heard from Obama. Then Obama's bold move was to send Hillary to Geneva for international talks. There was supposed to be a whole lot of reasoning with other countries that would fix the problem. Meanwhile, while Obama and Hillary are waxing philosophical and ever so wordy, murders are happening and America is NOT leading.

Oh…did I tell you yet that this week Obama has doing great at golf and had fun picking his favorite NCAA teams. Who cares if Japan and the Middle East are in melt down…golf caddy, please.

Once Obama got the 600 Americans out of Libya he still stalled as our allies led. British Prime Minister Cameron and French President Sarkozy were first to call for a no-fly zone. All this, while Obama and Hillary say they have delayed because they don't want to appear like they are trying to take Libyan oil.

Obama and Hillary don't want to appear to the Muslim world like they are extreme or that they would steal oil. Isn't that special? Maybe they both need therapy. They sure wouldn't want to develop the dreaded…."Muslim appearism-aphobia."

This administration is doing it again…too little, too late. We saw the Obama administration give passive and empty words to the Green movement in Iran in 2009, who were courageously marching in the streets against the evil tyrant Mahmoud Ahmadinejad. Hundreds were killed and arrested while we passively watched. Obama made a barely audible rebuke to the president's treatment of the masses rising up and standing for freedom. That was it! That was our time to move quickly, lead and stop the murders. We didn't need the U.N. or Mommy to tell us what to do. That was America's opportunity to defend freedom and rise up against this aggressive and evil tyrant and help to unseat him. We failed.

Now, we have seen the Middle East light on fire all over. Thousands in many Muslim countries are rising up and courageously putting their lives on the line to taste freedom. This is not only about the importance of standing boldly for those wanting freedom, but also about standing for our national security. It is a deadly danger for America to sit back and continue to be passive as Islamic countries implode because of groups like the Muslim Brotherhood and other radicals waiting to swoop in and take over. The Islamic world is radical enough without us sitting back and saying it is basically none of our business, while they become more radical and dangerous to anyone who is different.

What have we seen from the Obama administration? In response to Egypt's uprising, Obama quickly backed off support for long standing ally Hosni Mubarak (not a perfect guy, I know), and siding with the radical Muslim Brotherhood who has been circling their wagons to lead this "moderate" Muslim country that has nuclear capability.

We see Obama concerned more about wrong perceptions and

appearing extreme to the Muslim world, so we won't act in a timely manner to stop the murders in Libya. In fact, the world is told that we won't act first on this and that is supposed to win us points.

Last year we saw the passive and total loss of a golden opportunity to get things going in the right direction in Iran by supporting the Greens and now all we hear from Obama as usual are words, words and more words. Let's talk, stall, discuss and wait. That is his plan for international leadership for America.

Obama is dangerous, ineffective, cowardly, and most Un-American. The nation must rise up and vote him out in 2012. We have a lot of repair work to do here and abroad, but first we have to get our principles back into shape and our constitutional vision back in line as to who we are. Join me on my show and let me know what you think. www.therothshow.com.

America Must Stand For Freedom And Human Rights Again

I'm the first to understand that America shouldn't meddle in everything and try and control the world. However, if we truly believe that freedom is a gift and right given from God, and in what our constitution says, we have to stand against evil and murderers. We can't wax philosophical and mildly concerned while other people's right to simply stay alive is stolen in front of our eyes. We have to do what is right though the cost be inconvenient, not good for politics and even bloody.

Women, Freedom And Human Rights

What about the endless struggle of women's rights and freedom? In the Holy Bible times we saw women written about who ran businesses, were enterprising and did ministry. Then there was Esther. She was made queen and saved the entire nation of Israel. She did this as an orphan raised by her uncle and kidnapped to a pagan king's palace to be showcased with hundreds of seized women. The pagan king planned to choose a new queen. She didn't exactly have a great start in life, knowing the right people, having the right money and drawing strength from her parents. She simply trusted in and relied on God for guidance and help. She did remarkable things because with God all things are possible and she trusted Him.

The last several thousand years there have seen women rise up in bold leadership and achievement in spite of profound challenges and limitations many of them faced. Look at what vision, passion and a little talent has done. These are a few of my favorite women:

Joan of Arc 1412-1431

Joan of Arc was the 17 year old who received "heavenly visions" believing she was to lead the French in revolt against the control of the English. The most unlikely heroine, she did just that. She led the French to victory at Orleans. Later she was arrested and burned at the stake. Look what a spiritually connected teenage girl did to lead her whole country to victory.

Catherine the Great 1729-1796

She was one of the greatest political leaders in the eighteenth century. She made Russia one of the most successful and dominant countries in Europe, improved life for Russian serfs and developed the arts. She served and loved her country.

Harriet Beecher Stowe 1811-1896

This lady was gutsy and amazing. She campaigned nearly her whole life against slavery. Perhaps you have read her bestseller,

Uncle Tom's Cabin, which made popular the anti-slavery campaign. Even Abraham Lincoln remarked that her books became a big factor behind the civil war in America.

Susan B. Anthony 1820-1906

Susan also campaigned against slavery, but also for women's and worker's rights. She was passionate about the importance of women having the right to vote and traveled around the country giving untold speeches to that effect. She was one of the major forces leading this country in the right direction regarding worker's rights, women's rights and putting another spike in the evil heart of slavery.

Helen Keller 1880-1968

Helen became deaf and blind at 19 months of age. She struggled to overcome and thrive while losing all sight and hearing. She worked and campaigned her whole life to help, inspire and encourage those who were also deaf and blind.

Rosa Parks 1913-2005

We remember Rosa for refusing to give up her seat on a bus to a white man. Her guts and example led to the most significant legislation protecting civil rights in American history. She was humble, playing down her role in the civil rights battles, but her impact was huge, and courage rare.

Mother Teresa 1910-1997

How could we forget the nun who felt led by God to devote her whole life to the extremely poor, sick, and dying in Calcutta. She became a global example showing us God's heart to care for those neglected by society.

Margaret Thatcher 1925 –

Margaret Thatcher, the first female Prime Minister of Great

Britain, holding power for a decade. I remember her has leading the fight for individual responsibility and belief in free markets. She fought against the integration of Europe into the EU. She was a close friend of Ronald Reagan and stood for freedom and sovereignty.

Benazir Bhutto 1953-2007

A bold woman of courage, Benazir Bhutto was the first female prime minister of a Muslim country. That was a huge miracle and breakthrough in a male-dominated Muslim world. She took Pakistan from a dictatorship to a democracy in 1977. Later on she was accused of corruption, but to this day denies it.

Dorothy Hodgkin 1910-1994

Some of you are alive today because of Dorothy Hodgkin's contribution. She was awarded the Nobel Prize for chemistry. Her investigations and findings led to the creation of penicillin and later on, insulin. We know what these discoveries have done for improvements in health care. She was a crusader for health care her entire life.

There are untold examples worldwide of women, taking hold of bigger visions than themselves and accomplishing the seemingly impossible. Women have been key players in fighting for and getting voting rights for women, conquering slavery and ensuring civil rights, leading whole countries to freedom, eradicating disease, fighting on the front lines against tyranny, making musical, dramatic and academic history, pushing through the walls of disability to victory, and being the carrier of compassion and kindness to the disenfranchised. Any questions?

Islam And Women's Rights

Not everyone or every institution is honoring women's value and rights however. I challenge Islam to do some major review and house cleaning in this area if they want to stand along side the West and free world in peace.

What will Islam do about this and their treatment of women around the world?

Quran in Sura 2:223 says:

Your women are your fields, so go into your fields whichever way you like …

Quran in Sura 2:228 says:

…Wives have the same rights as the husbands have on them in accordance with the generally known principles. Of course, men are a degree above them in status…

Quran in Sura 4:11 says:

The share of the male shall be twice that of a female…

Quran in Sura 2:282 says:

And let two men from among you bear witness to all such documents (contracts of loans without interest). But if two men be not available, there should be one man and two women to bear witness so that if one of the women forgets (anything), the other may remind her.

Quran in Sura 2:230 says:

And if the husband divorces his wife (for the third time), she shall not remain his lawful wife after this (absolute) divorce, unless she marries another husband and the second husband divorces her. In that case there is no harm if they (the first couple) remarry…

Quran in Sura 4:24 says:

And forbidden to you are wedded wives of other people except those who have fallen in your hands (as prisoners of war)...

Quran in Sura 4:3 says:

And if you be apprehensive that you will not be able to do justice to the orphans, you can marry two or three or four women whom you choose. But if you apprehend that you might not be able to do justice to them, then marry only one wife, or marry those who have fallen in your possession.

Quran in Sura 4: 129 says:

It is not within your power to be perfectly equitable in your treatment with all your wives, even if you wish to be so; therefore, in order to satisfy the dictates of Divine Law do not lean towards one wife so as to leave the other in a state of suspense.

Quran in Sura 4:34 says:

....If you fear highhandedness from your wives, remind them of the teaching of God, then ignore them when you go to bed, then hit them. If they obey you, you have not right to act against them. God is most high and great.

Quran in Sura 65.1,4 says:

(65:1): O Prophet, when you (and the believers) divorce women, divorce them for their prescribed waiting-period and count the waiting–period accurately....

(65:4) And if you are in doubt about those of your women who have despaired of menstruation, (you should know that) their waiting period is three months, and the same applies to those who have not menstruated as yet. As for pregnant women, their period ends when they have delivered their burden.

Dig and educate yourself on what the Quran says regarding treatment of women. Find out more at: http://infidelsarecool.com, www. jihadwatch.org, www.iqalrasooli.com. Look up the verses directly in the Quran if you think I am lying.

There are over 1.6 billion Muslims in the world today. What are the Muslims in leadership going to do with the hundreds of millions of women within their religious and cultural structure? Will visionaries and leaders rise up to stand against the blatant mistreatment of women within Islam? Or will the free world learn more and more about what the Quran says and how Islamic women are treated?

Promoting marriage and sex with prepubescent girls, beating of wives, describing women as a field to be plowed, a woman's testimony valued as half of a man, sex required of a woman no matter how she feels or what she wants, on and on.

I challenge Islam to confront and get real with women's rights and dare to confront their own internal demons that chronically abuse and mistreat women.

While Islam is confronting the vivid abuse against women, they must take on the broad abuse of Sharia law and confront its rights violating core that calls for the killing of those who convert to another faith, execution of gay people, beating of wives, cutting off of hands for robbers, and more. How many times have I heard of a rape victim in an Islamic country being whipped within an inch of her life. Blame the victim if it is a woman - most common in Sharia law.

I understand that there are all kinds of religions in the world and they all think they have the way. People make personal decisions on their faith for a variety of reasons. We will all stand before God with our decision on faith and choice in this life. Let us make sure we make the right one and don't just attach to a handed down tradition. Why do you believe what you believe? Think it through and ask every question you can. Your very eternity might depend on it.

Value Of Life

Our precious Declaration of Independence declares that we are endowed by our Creator with certain unalienable rights, that among these are Life, Liberty and the pursuit of Happiness. Notice the first right listed among many is the right to life. That is precisely why that life must be protected and honored from the womb on up through adulthood.

This nation has screamed and yelled forever about "pro life" "pro choice" issues. Do we abort? do we not abort? Legal fight this, and legal fight that. "I don't want government on my body, though I think abortion is bad." "Women's rights, women's choices...." "It's not a baby until...." I have heard it all for years.

Obama is the most abortion-supporting President of all time. Well before he was elected into the White House, he voted for several abortion bills, including infanticide. He didn't even want a survivor of an abortion lying on a table to get medical help. Just let the baby lie there in misery and die. That is our President.

Abortion is wrong to me because life is unique, precious and a gift from God. The baby forms rather quickly in the womb in the first three months and looks like a baby. It was always obvious to me it was a baby growing in a woman's womb, not a head of lettuce that magically becomes a human baby at month nine.

Life is unique and should be protected at the youngest age and the oldest. Who will defend the rights of the young baby? What about their "right to life" as the Declaration of Independence states?

Slaughtering babies in the womb for whatever reason is the complete violation of their right to life and is murder. It doesn't matter whether a baby needs help staying alive or not. Don't all babies and young toddlers need parental help to eat, survive and live well after birth also?

If life in the womb was important to the great President Ronald Reagan, that is good enough for me. You have to ask the bottom line question. Where does life come from? It comes from Almighty God. A baby must not be destroyed when countless people would die to adopt a baby if a Mom didn't feel like she could raise it. My husband and I couldn't have children so we foster/adopted both our kids. Obviously, two other family situations didn't work out but ours did. Our kids are most happy to be alive and have a family.

Human worth and freedom must not be challenged and severed by any person, any religion or any government. God made us all in his image, every sex, every race, everyone. The grand design was for us to be drawn to God, love Him and each other. I believe He miraculously did this through His amazing gift of Jesus Christ, who gave all so we might have life and live abundantly.

The first freedom God gave mankind was freedom to choose. We can choose to love and believe in Him or not. It is our choice and the consequences therein. If God Himself gives people the freedom to choose and make decisions, how then can we not allow people the freedom to be, as we wrestle through life's issues.

Freedom and Judeo-Christian values are what have made America great. It has led her to become the leader of the Free World. Of all the things we all fight about…freedom and our right to live is one of the few things actually worth fighting for.

Chapter 6
ILLEGAL IMMIGRATION BORDER SECURITY

Securing our borders and stopping the flow of illegal aliens, drugs and potential terrorists has been argued, screamed and yelled about for several decades. What are all the hot button issues thrown out?

We hear that it is "Family values": referring to families coming illegally across the border to get ahead for their families. Then we hear illegal aliens are simply doing jobs Americans won't do anyway.

Along with all those coming across our borders for "family values" sake and to find a job, there are countless more who are committing other crimes, such as drug dealing, identity theft, terrorism, robbery and sex crimes. There are illegal aliens who end up in gangs in cities across the country and thousands end up in our prisons. In fact, one third of our prison population is said to be of illegal alien status.

We have $200 billion going back and forth each year in drug money between America and Mexico. In addition to the out of control drug war going on, there have been several near misses and close calls with Islamic terrorists who have snuck in or tried to sneak in and do us harm.

Michael Carlin, editor of Century City News in L.A., told me that an Iranian diplomat was caught setting up weapon supply lines a few years back, all the way from Nicaragua up to L.A. He got caught when he didn't turn in his rental car and a service person at the rental car place noticed his Spanish was bad. Just what did he have in mind? He was certainly not planning a Bible Study.

I don't recall a President for the last few decades that did more than talk about this dangerous and growing problem to the country. Estimates range from 10-40 million illegal aliens living in America. Counties, states, schools, and hospitals have and are going bankrupt simply dealing with the multimillions of added financial and service burdens burying them.

Meanwhile, as jobs are stolen on a grand scale from Americans, greedy U.S. businesses look the other way and illegally hire them for cheap labor, while our government picks and chooses when to force immigration law already on the books. Rarely do rogue employers get fined and penalized for hiring illegal aliens. It is a vicious and out of control cycle. Illegal aliens from all over come across our border. American businesses will hire them and rarely will our laws confront them or their employer.

Estimates vary, but FAIR (Fairness & Accuracy In Reporting) Research shows troubling info we should be concerned about. An estimated 1,880,000 American workers lose jobs every year due to illegal immigration. In addition, the cost of providing welfare and assistance to Americans out of work, who have lost low-skill jobs, is over $15 billion a year.

The bottom line is that multibillions are being spent each year to service Americans who can't get entry level jobs, service illegal aliens who apply and get all kinds of state and federal assistance, and one third of these aliens end up in our prisons, another massive expense. $60 billion dollars are sent home by illegal aliens to Mexico each year. Next to exports and oil sales this is Mexico's largest revenue stream. The way things have been handled for years with Mexico now by the U.S. government certainly doesn't stop this madness in a real manner.

We just talk, then disappear, talk some more and have coffee, talk some more and go to dinner. It is high time to really do something, which addresses the many sides to this massive issue.

This stupid co-dependency and violation to America dramatically feeds our $200 billion a year drug flow and trade, while increasing our chance for a major attack from a Muslim radical who slips through. They are no doubt here and awaiting orders already.

We have seen the great President Ronald Reagan think he was doing the right thing and offer amnesty to 12-15 million illegal aliens at the time in 1986. He thought that would actually reduce the flow of illegal aliens. It only sky-rocketed it and acted like a neon invitation sign. Since then various Presidents have talked about amnesty but now it rings like extreme Leftist schemes to grab Hispanic votes and screw the American people, economy and jobs.

Most of us have a heart of compassion but don't see how rewarding sneaky and criminal behavior helps any of us. So what on earth do we do…round them up somehow and put them in cattle cars to blast back to Mexico? Some do say that or something like that is the answer, but at what expense and how does this actually stop the flow coming in?

I have wrestled with the back and forth of this problem for years and after looking at so many sides of it I finally found a plan offered up by Michael Carlin, editor of the *Century City News* in LA. He calls his plan, the "Why Not Plan", www.whynotplan.info. When he first came on my radio show and introduced the idea I was cautiously intrigued. I asked him all the devil's advocate questions, then started believing this could indeed be the answer if implemented with the right leadership.

I believe the "Why not Plan", authored by Michael Carlin, addresses accountability, national security, compassion, jobs and law. It covers the bases in an entrepreneurial, fresh, non-political way, and frankly, it is about time. This is the plan I would implement if I were President.

First things first: Secure the border for real. Put the National Guard on the border with real authority. Give more and consistent authority back to the Border Patrol as well. Along with the thousands of Military and Border Patrol support up and down the border, we could enact an improved upon and expanded virtual fence and in some areas a real fence. Complementing all this would be advanced satellite techniques and surveillance. Securing our border can and must be done. We have just never had the will to do it. We have only touched on it and almost given lip service. Not OK anymore.

Once the borders are finally secured with all drug, terrorist and illegal alien traffic stopped, then we would want to invite and court the illegal aliens out of the hidden shadows. If they came out within 90 days, they would be required to really identify themselves, not with just one I.D. or a fake I.D. We would need to know they were not a criminal, terrorist or someone else hiding here. Once they had come forth and were known, then they would be invited on a two-year track toward amnesty after two verifiable years of legal and tax-paying behavior. They would also be required to learn English.

If an illegal alien came in within six months they would be on a four-year plan toward amnesty. After six months and no response, if found, they would be deported and not allowed back.

While we would be extending a new form of amnesty over time, after verifying who they are and staying clean, we would be building what Carlin calls the Honor Zone which would be a 50-80 mile zone of land on the Mexican side that would include U.S. businesses who wanted to operate there and hire Mexican workers for Mexican rates. America would win because big business would get the cheaper labor many of them crave, and Mexico would win because their people would get work and stay home. Hopefully, as the Honor zone built up, protected by the Mexican military, this would also draw illegal aliens down from the US mainland to work there.

We must finally have the will to secure our borders, back our troops and Border Patrol on the borders, find out who is hiding and working in America, either send them back or put them on a plan we define and monitor, then create real opportunity for American business to thrive and Mexican workers to work in the Honor zone on the Mexican side.

Chapter 7
COMMON SENSE

Over the years of doing my radio show, writing my articles and being a Mom, there have been many things that just seem like plain old common sense to me. I can't figure out why so many politicians ruin so much and make things so complicated. It seems like most of them have talent, though, that is, a talent for demolition.

The following things are just common sense to me.

Guns

People have the right to keep and bear arms. Our founders and Constitution gave us Second Amendment rights for a reason and last I checked, guns don't kill people, people do. If a bad guy decides that you are going to die, they will do whatever it takes to get you or try to. That means grabbing a knife in the kitchen, a club in the garage, backing the car over you, choking you with their hands, burning your house down, poisoning you, hiring someone to beat you up and kill you or getting a gun and shooting you.

More draconian controls on guns, their usage and sales, won't stop danger and crimes. Why? Because the bad guys get guns illegally, anyway. They could care less about regulations and licenses. They will get what they need if they want it, by stealing. So why do the gun control people think that putting more restrictions and regulations on guns and their usage will lower crime? Brady law this, and gun control that. All this does is take guns away or make them much more difficult to get, from law abiding people who would like to protect their family, property and self. Remember, the bad guys will always get their guns in their own way.

Just go to Gun Owners of America or the NRA and you can find info on crime rates and cities in our country. Has gun control worked?

In Maryland, who banned small handguns that people could actually afford, they had their murder rate go up 20 percent.

New Hampshire has almost zero gun control laws and it is considered one of the safest places to live in the country.

The Future of Freedom Foundation's, ***Freedom Daily***, has a great article by Benedict D. LaRosa that highlights very revealing gun stats that you would think would get the point across to all the gun control people. ("The Illogic of Gun Controllers", Benedict D. LaRosa, F.F.F. Freedom Daily, May 12, 2010 www.fff.org/freedom/fd1002f.asp.)

Some of these simple facts include:

Those states that have passed concealed-carry laws have seen their murder rate fall by 8.5 percent, rapes by 5 percent, aggravated assaults by 7 percent and robbery by 3 percent.

The vivid example is of Texas, who had one of the worst crime rates in the country, 38 percent higher than the national average in the 1990s. Once they voted in the concealed-carry law in 1994, everything changed. Their crime rate dropped 50 percent faster than the whole nation. Hello, anyone home? Crime is much lower in state after state where law-abiding citizens can own guns easier and carry concealed weapons.

It is common sense to tell government to get its paws of our guns, especially in our cities. Crimes go down in every city where the law-abiding citizens have more guns.

Education

As a Mom I am all for schools being invested in safety and providing relevant classes for our children. I am not for schools being transformed into immoral, environmentally appropriate, anti-Historical and anti-Christian training zones however.

I support the promotion of at least one constitutional and founding documents class in every public grade school, middle school and high school. This should be supported by teaching our REAL history, the good, bad and ugly of it. As it is now however, there is way more distorted history being taught. Our kids are taught the distorted, frankly, communist view of "sustainability" and are taught to practically live in shame due to "presented" history. We must teach our children and adults the truth about the miracle of our founding, how God really was a part of the creation of our nation and how we have fought for what is good in our country and around the world. We really do live in the only country on earth that has a constitution, history and achievement like ours. It is not arrogance to be proud of America and to take good care of her.

We need to promote core basics and restore parents' rights with regard to having the right to know about their child getting pregnant and/or pursuing an abortion. As it is now, some schools have stated that a kid can sneak out and have an abortion without informing their parent. That is dead wrong. It is not only a total violation to parents' rights and authority over their child, but dangerous to a child in many ways. Abortion has been shown to have all kinds of risks with it, from internal bleeding, severe depression or other medical complications. What if something life threatening happened while an abortion was happening and the parents knew nothing about it?

That certainly isn't sane or common sense.

Who Is Special In Schools?

I think public schools should push for a day for all kids to be special. That means every unique kid in the school, not just a certain race, gay kid or other classification. Aren't they all special and unique, whether they are black, white, Hispanic, gay, straight, fat, skinny, popular, unpopular, cross-eyed, foster adopted, disabled or some other variety?

Why should the few gay kids get a special day as opposed to everyone else who is also special?

Education is where our kids spend a good chunk of their life until they are 18. We should not only push for an excellent education with real and relevant classes, but allow choice in where families choose to send their kids. This will create competition and promote excellence. School can never be a place for political or environmental indoctrination.

State and Federal Sovereignty

There is a growing swell in the country to recognize our states' rights. You may not recall or be aware of just how much power and authority each state has, even over the intrusion of the federal government. State leadership all across the country is starting to get a clue and taking stands against draconian federal programs, such as Obama's tax-laden, oppressive, mandated health care that has rocked our country.

We saw Judge Vincent out of Florida rule against Obama's health care bill, saying it was completely unconstitutional and couldn't fly.

He represented 26 states that were standing against this for their Tenth Amendment rights. We saw the House vote to repeal it but naturally the Senate, Liberal-controlled, voted it down. The House knew they would have to go to battle plan B, defunding it, which they are. It will be a longer process, but they can and must continue to defund it, take it apart and crush it. If allowed to prevail on the American people, it would be a complete disaster and ruin the best health care system in the world and seriously violate our rights and constitution.

Obama could care less about states' rights. He stood against Governor Walker in Wisconsin, trying his best to come up with an honorable compromise with unions who were demanding big money their way. All this when the state was practically bankrupt and everyone who had a brain had to give somewhere. Instead of supporting common sense and fair play with the unions and Governor Walker's negotiations, he kissed up to the extreme…as usual.

We also watched Obama step all over states' rights when he sued the State of Arizona and Governor Jan Brewer, another brave and excellent Governor, who voted in a much needed illegal immigration law. They lead with home invasions in the country, and have out of control crime and budget horror due to out of control illegal aliens coming across the border. Our President not only sued the governor and the state, he aligned with a foreign government, Mexico, to add betrayal to the lawsuit. The predictable and final betrayal of the Obama Administration was to take this much needed decision, voted in by the majority of the people in a sovereign state, was to go to the U.N. about it wanting further punishment.

I find it interesting in as much as President Obama does not stand for states' rights, this may very well be his undoing in 2012, since at least 12 states are pushing hard to put laws on the books to require proof of citizenship to run for President. Even if only 3-4 pass, imagine him getting no votes in those states since he wouldn't be on the ballot if he still refused to show his long form birth certificate. The very states' rights he detests by his actions, are the very rights that might just boot him out.

Real Health Care reform

There needs to be real health care national conversations, debates and reform. Reform that actually makes sense will allow even more competition with private and public hospitals. It will pursue portability across state lines with job changes and torte reform. Out of control and greedy lawsuits make health care insurance and hospital care too expensive for all of us.

If I were President and we had our $8 trillion wallet of tax money to operate from, I would propose adding another $200 billion to Medicare, Medicaid and CHIPS, to make sure treatment was excellent, timely and paid for (remember, at least $3.5 trillion would be chunking down our debt each year). We cannot compromise care for our seniors, those with disabilities and special needs. I would also propose a national program for the sake of baseline health and national security, a free immunization program to be offered to lessen the blow of the flu season, and foreign invaders that threaten many in society.

If there was real leadership in the White House you could face-lift medical care in the U.S. like you can't even imagine. We can do this without forcing anything on anyone, taxing anyone, shredding capitalism and competition, and rationing care to our seniors and most needy.

How Would I Deal With Sharia Law?

As President of the United States, I would be the first President to boldly state what Sharia law states and pushes throughout Muslim countries. I would ask and campaign to Middle East leaders and all Muslim leaders to enact visible and swift reforms with Sharia. As it is now, those who convert to other faiths are executed, wives are regularly beaten by their husbands, gays are executed, limbs are cut off for stealing and women are whipped because they have been raped if they don't have four witnesses. That behavior does not just represent another religious opinion, but is evil and must stop. I would push for legislation not only to ban Sharia ever from being considered in anyway in the U.S. or our courts, but ask for and expect Muslim leadership to demonstrate these reforms to the U.N., media and world.

I would promote bold sanctions, stopping trade, purchases of oil and other commodities if they chose to continue these vile and abusive practices within Islamic countries. Anyone with an ounce of decency and common sense, regardless of their religious point of view, should know you don't whip rape victims and execute people for being gay or changing their faith.

Instead of our leaders current and past showing real leadership on this international distortion and evil, we seem desperately meek and tilted on this, no doubt because of our dependence on getting over 50 percent of our oil from OPEC nations. We should have never allowed ourselves to be dependent on so much foreign oil.

That distorts our Middle East decisions and frankly, is a crime to the U.S. and world.

Maybe other Presidents won't, but I will stand for Muslim women's rights. I'll also say it right here and now as a conservative Christian, straight woman. I have never been for gay marriage, but I will stand between any executioner and any gay person. That is an evil crime. We can argue, scream, yell, and vote this in and that in, but we don't threaten and murder people who are different!

Women's Rights

This has been a humongous battle and movement with roots back to the beginning of our nation and culture. Women have come a long way in the U.S. Thankfully, we had bold women in the suffrage movement who fought for our rights until we could vote and lead.

To me, women's rights come from God, as do men's rights. It is common sense in my view to show respect and fair ball to both sexes and all races. We are all special and unique before we are a man or woman. Didn't God make us all, and demonstrate men and women in leadership throughout the Bible and in cultures that have worked? There should be no top dog and no underdog. That is why when Sharia states that women's vote is valued in court as half of a man's, and that a man is worth a degree more than a woman…there is something rotten going on.

I am the first person to stand for equal pay for equal work. Opportunities are available to both sexes, while acknowledging uniquely male and female characteristics and gender. We are all unique, but I do think men are a bit different then women. That is all good, and varies from person to person, thus the need to be fair to all and open doors for all.

A big area that some women, I believe, confuse women's rights and freedom with is abortion. Of all groups to lift up human rights and to protect the uniqueness of life it should be women. The Right to Life is the first major right listed in the Declaration of Independence. I understand as a woman there is a nine month commitment and journey a woman takes when she is pregnant, but if for some reason she doesn't want the baby or thinks she can't have it, that baby doesn't magically morph into a head of lettuce or amoeba. It is a young child, who is just as dependent, more so, in the womb as it is during the first few years after birth. No matter how desperate or stressed you might feel about having an unplanned pregnancy, killing the child inside you is still murder. Yes, God can forgive you and you can move on, but your child, and his or her right to life, cannot.

I challenge women to really lead and lift up the banner of life and moral choice regardless of their race, political persuasion and preference. To help fix our country and this world, we must put life back in the category it belongs: Youngest to the oldest - precious; all races - precious; all people regardless of behavior, faith or background - precious. When we finally begin to see all people as God sees us, with love and worth, this world will begin to change.

Minority Rights

Thank God, we have finally moved in the right direction and slapped racism upside the head. We had major battles with the civil war, then civil rights era, but we made it and must continue to heal and grow. We have plenty of work to still do, since some out there still want to dominate or abuse another because they have a different color. Thankfully, we have seen African Americans lead all over the political arena. Just a few I can think of the top of my head include; four-star general and former Secretary of State, Colin Powell; another Secretary of State, Condoleezza Rice; war hero and now congressman, Colonel Allen West; diplomat, Alan Keyes; and U.S. Supreme Court Justice, Clarence Thomas. Let alone that now we have a black President. Though I don't agree with Obama's decisions and worldview and would stand against him on principle, I am thrilled that America in good faith was at the stage where they could vote for a black man. Perhaps we are now moving into a time where a person of any race could get elected, or a woman could get elected, not on color or sex, but on ideas, vision and ability. Bring it on.

We need to put some common sense in our brains regarding race. Whites aren't all good, and whites aren't all bad. Same with Blacks, Hispanics, Asians and every other race. Our goodness and uniqueness comes out when we treat each other as someone made and loved by God Himself who has a plan and purpose for each life. We must practice loving in order to really learn to love and make change.

Budgets Need To Be Sane

Just because we transition to a 2 percent sales tax and no other, doesn't mean it is time to waste even more money and ignore our debt. Real leadership should get rid of redundancy in federal budgets that duplicates and wastes taxpayer's money. Budgets should also reflect ethics and national goals, not local, special interest and trendy goals. We need sanity infused again in spending. Instead, we have seen in time of a national recession and nearly $15 trillion in out of control debt, we study condom use with prostitutes in China, build bridges to nowhere and underground turtle tunnels.

We will save a whole lot of money, become energy independent, get major tax relief and stand up to the real bad guys, if we put a Mom in the White House and not another politician. This Mom, anyway, tends to cut to the bottom line. I don't have time to play political theatre and games.

Gay Rights

Gay and abortion issues seem to freak everyone out. My position on gay issues is simple. We are a country with Judeo-Christian values and a strong moral heritage. That is our successful skeletal structure and core. This is the part that has made us a great nation and blessed us. Marriage is defined in our country and every country in the world as between a man and a woman. This has long standing Christian roots, inspired from the Holy Bible, but also a long history and cultural tradition for the sake of societal and family stability.

I understand we have gay people in America who want to feel safe and experience freedom; that is completely understandable. Gays already have all the precious rights of a U.S. citizen, can love who they want, live with who they want, pick what ever career they feel inspired to pursue and have the talent to achieve, and be who they are. I pity gay people who find themselves in Muslim country and get discovered. That is a death sentence many times. Thank God for how America treats people of difference. Scream, yell, and vote people in and out, campaign and debate, that is the American way, not violence, torture and murder.

If I were President, I would support gays getting civil unions but not marriage, since it is a long standing religious and cultural tradition that protects the family and societal structure in my view.

I have had a lot of gay friends and love many, but not as "gay." They are unique people whom I met mostly when I was in the music business. I am not for mainstreaming gay behavior as "normal", "just another lifestyle", "the same as Mommy and Daddy" in a family system and "no choice" in the matter. However, gays are citizens, have every right to live their life, choose their lover, get a civil union and feel safe. That does not mean rewrite and manipulate school curriculum, mainstreet it as totally acceptable and normal to all, especially most parents, Christians and Conservatives.

We can however, work together, love each other, support each other where we can, and talk through many of the issues, even as we might disagree.

Chapter 8
WHY IS DR. LAURIE ROTH THE BEST CANDIDATE

I Have Real Things To Accomplish, Not Political Sound Bites And Name Calling

Obama and the progressive leftists are doing exactly what we would expect desperate people to do; name call, create enemies, cultivate crises and try to distract. Don't you just love how so many conservatives are "witches", "deviants", "want to destroy or stop social security", "hate poor people and illegal aliens", on and on. Along with all the name calling and slander flinging by the left are the absurd heroic and persecution portrayals of Obama.

I was stunned after the Chilean miner disaster and scare we heard Harry Reid in a speech in Nevada comparing Obama to the Chilean Miners in his focus and heroism. "It was like the Chilean miners, but he, being the man he is, rolled up his sleeves and said "I am going to get us out of this hole." (Senator Harry Reid (D-NV).) Is Obama going to be compared to Mother Theresa soon?

Think back to the midterm elections that made history when the Conservatives, Tea Party people, and Independents dramatically shifted the House to the right. In one of Obama's midterm pitch talks he said, "The Empire is Striking Back." Think about this statement for a minute. Just what does "the Empire" mean in his mind? The empire is "the people" apparently, the "scared", fearful, "non-objective people" who are responding against him out of stress. That would explain our actions and his lowering poll numbers right? WRONG!

Darth Vader is not only back and very angry, but hundreds of millions of Darth Vaders are also mobilized and not happy. Obama can call us whatever he wants. We know the truth. Obama is the real Darth Vader and is trying to turn us into an Evil Empire. We aren't the Empire at all, he, his czars, Progressive Leftists and Socialist Liberals in the Senate and House are.

The American people will rise up in the 2012 elections and stop Obama Empire's movement and plans. They can talk all they want about the fear, stress, and crisis-type reactions of the American people but it won't matter now. We will do what we have to do to fix and save our country, bring back our freedom and way of life. Nothing this President and congress has stood for and campaigned for has defended our constitution, Judeo-Christian values and freedoms. Obama has instead attacked and challenged them all.

Obama can pick his movie. If he needs us to be the "Empire Striking Back", the "tornado" that lifts up Dorothy's house and places it in Oz, or the stars of that classic movie, "Ground Hog Day" where everything repeats itself each day, consider it done. Just know that in truth, the American and Constitutional Empire is "Striking Back", the Progressive /Leftist house has been ripped off its foundation by an outraged tornado and will fly away soon. We started the house-cleaning and process in the midterms. We will finish the job in 2012.

I Am The Real Communicator -
In Fact My Ph.D. Is In Counseling

What was Obama's response to the GOP slaughter in the House? "It's just a communication and messaging problem."

You can't write this stuff in movies. During the obvious political and American backlash against the Obama and congressional dictatorship, we heard Pelosi saying the Democrats would keep the House, agendas and health care would continue and Obama and the big vision were just fine. Wasn't that optimism precious? Pelosi should consider becoming a fiction writer. She demonstrates a rare form of understanding with fantasy and creativity. Maybe she should consider a Botox franchise. That wasn't even nice, I know.

Not only has Obama and his wacky Progressive (former) heads minimized every tanking poll and anger of the American people, Obama was said to have not even watched or paid attention to the midterm election night. I guess Mr. Coolness was above that or had a rock concert to go to. If any of you actually believe Obama didn't track the elections on that fateful night, then ice cubes grow in hell.

The political backlash against Obama and the Progressives in Congress couldn't have possibly been due to any of the following:

Forcing the American people to have government-sanctioned health care insurance or else massive fines and threats from the controlling IRS.

Spending and wasting several trillion dollars in stimulus and health care "control dollars."

Apologizing for and about America and her real history to leaders all over the world, especially Muslim leaders.

Placing nearly 40 czars in place to bypass Congress and accountability; only answering to Obama as they plan to control and regulate the snot out of almost every quadrant of American life and business.

Showing a continued, lame, and late response regarding national security threats, e.g., three day delay regarding the Underwear Christmas bomber, supporting the building of a 13 story Mosque, promoted and funded by radical Muslims (follow the trail Douglas Hagmann exposed on my show), doing a moronic nuclear treaty with Russia, giving billions to terrorist group, Hamas, and more.

Obama has continuously insulted conservatives, Christians, Republicans and the growing Tea Party gatherings. We have a juicy potluck of insults we are collecting…Birthers, racists, empire striking back, hostage takers, enemies, domestic terrorists…it just keeps coming.

Insisting on the pursuit of Cap and Trade, global warming fantasy, carbon emissions and environmental distortion. Even though science, reality, and the American people pointed boldly against this, Obama and the U.N. wanted the international tax and environmental controls to be put in place. This agenda alone, if left, would cause America several more trillion dollars in damage and ruination.

Obama has lied from day one about trying to fix the economy and creating jobs and relief for the American people. He plans to undo the Bush tax cuts and give everyone a tax increase. There are at least 20 hidden taxes also in the health care plan.

Starting a war with Libya and bypassing Congress.

The list of betrayals and failures by this President and Progressives could flood a sea of pages. The bottom line is that the American people have not only noticed the endless insults, lies and betrayals to our Constitution, our Judeo-Christian values and freedoms, we no longer intend to take it, thus the major spankage we saw in the last midterms.

As the jobless claims were rising ever higher, our President decided on just one of his many vacations and trips abroad, he would take his worshipping and defeated entourage to India for a three day visit. Thirty-four war ships went over to protect his "star appeal" butt, and this cost us $200 million a day. He requested a fleet of limousines; almost all of his White House staff went as well. They booked 800 rooms in the Taj and Hyatt Hotels. Isn't that special?

The bottom line is, other than transforming this country into a socialist/communist and Liberal regime for Liberals, he has viewed his experience in the White House as power in entertaining, spending and fun. I have never heard of a President so obsessed with MTV-type interviews, concerts and $50-100 million dollar vacations for him and Michelle.

There has never once been a touch of concern about him hanging with the American people as they have really suffered and struggled through this depression/recession, losing jobs and homes as he has kept lying and spending.

When brought down, dictators never admit their failures and demise. There will be continued battles, ego and lies with Obama between now and 2012. He will be brought down, though. The house cleaning has already begun.

When we were promised such transparency and communication from Obama, I don't think any of us thought that "transparency" really meant "hidden and mysterious", and "communication" meant constant insults and slight of hand.

I Am Far From Perfect But I Am No Quitter And I Will Get All The Important Stuff Done Right

Ask my husband or closest friends about the real Laurie Roth and you will find I am not the best dresser, don't do my hair very well and will cheat on my socks every time. That part has been embar-

rassing a few times when I put on my old socks with holes in them
or that didn't match, and I had to fly somewhere to speak. Now days
at airport security, you get to have a modeling career displaying your
socks if not your bunions at security. Then of course you realize the
scam is over. You have been caught. The public now has proof you
aren't the "put together chick", but a tomboy posing as a traveling
professional…oh, well.

I am also not the best housekeeper. It's not that I don't clean, cook
and pick up stuff every day, but I have learned with kids not to sweat
the small stuff. Sometimes dust and a few piles in the corner can
just stay there until I am ready to deal with them. Every weekend,
it seems, I have a project in one room or another.

The truth is nobody, including moi, can get through every day
perfectly or with the best looking outfit or amazing accomplishments.
Sometimes in life the goal is simply to get out of bed, give the day to
God, and commit to doing the best you can. Don't hyperfocus on
what other people think, how cool or uncool you look today, and
what you can't do or haven't done.

Sometimes You Just Want To Quit

There are many types of "quitting." I have had it and can't take it
anymore, "I quit." Some of us quit because we are on our last nerve,
having endured at work, home or with a stressful situation for too
long. No doubt we have all done that in our life. Others quit as
a response to "practical" thinking and circumstances. There isn't
enough money coming in to continue, it takes too much energy and
time to continue…. Hanging in there won't give me any returns.
Others quit because they don't have or feel enough support from

those around them to continue a course.

On the "quitting scale" I would say I am the least likely to quit person I know. The dreams I have had and worked toward through out my life, music, radio, education, entertainment, helping others fulfill their dreams, working on TV shows and projects, have by and large been successful as I define success. Many of my goals are still a work in fluid progress.

After the first zillion attempts, I finally signed a record distribution deal with BMG distribution by thinking outside the box. I finally realized that the odds of some record mogul discovering me were around zero, so I discovered myself and signed myself to my own label, wrote my own promo sheets, put them in Billboard magazine and created a buzz. Soon, that got me on the cover of Cashbox magazine, then a big music trade, and I was represented by a big music promoter in 1995. I didn't sell the most records but I was out there in several countries, singing and living my dream. I eventually hosted and was one of the producers for a national TV show, **CD Highway**, which aired across the country on PBS for two seasons. There would have been no movement or record distribution at all if I had just quit when it was "practical" to do so. In fact, this year I am in touch with a producer who is planning to produce my next album. He has produced many platinum records for very famous singers.

Other Things I Didn't Quit On

Education: I also pushed my way through ten years of college to obtain a real Ph.D. in Counseling. I paid my way through, got an assistantship, and struggled, and I can guarantee you I didn't quit. I had no money in the bank, no benefactors and no rich parents. You can read my dissertation in the Oregon State Library. I have paid no money to hide my education. B.A., George Fox University; Masters in Counseling, Portland State University; Ph.D., Counseling, (emphasis, alcohol and drugs), Oregon State University. By the way, I have my birth certificate and was born at The Dalles Hospital in Oregon.

Life and Recovery: With the help of God, work, and prayer, I grabbed hold of a successful vision of recovery and healing I wanted. I then charted that course, worked hours a day to walk right, talk right, think right and see right. I realized shortly after I got home from the hospital after nearly two months there, that the outcome of what happened to me was actually up to me. God was waiting for my belief level and response, then He would match that and bring me that much further as I walked, worked and trusted Him.

Ten months after my near fatal motorcycle accident, I found a new engineer, call screener, new advertisers, new local station to air on in my home market and a small handful of others across the country who would pick me up again. I couldn't quite talk right, see right and I fought exhaustion but I started three hours a day again. I was with my same network, Information Radio Network. That was in June 2006. I had been off the air for ten months, and was very much yesterday's news, and most of my stations had long before signed other contracts. It really was like climbing Mount Everest with a bikini and no oxygen. Now, five years later, my show and markets are growing, I feel great and speak all over the country.

I Didn't Quit On Marriage And Family

After two broken engagements and struggling to meet the right guy, I went on line and found a dreamy guy on www.kiss.com, Rich. He was tall, dark and handsome, but also real. We were exact opposites; he was a neat freak, practical, manager type. He was picky to the point of annoying and I was casual and sloppy to the point of annoying. I was a big picture, creative, entrepreneurial type who didn't care how laundry was done. Rich did laundry a certain way and put things certain places. We fell in love anyway, trusted the Lord for the details and got married. We wanted to have kids and tried our hearts out but I couldn't get pregnant.

That was 11 years ago now and we have faced many trials and struggles together being so different and raising two kids we foster adopted, Mo at age 6 and Wayne at 14 months. Wayne is now 7 ½ and Mo is 14. The big hit that tested our marriage was my near fatal accident, which practically bankrupted us. Rich's pretty wife had suddenly turned into a drooling, Frankenstein who tripped everywhere. Rich stayed with me the whole time and worked his brains out to make the difference until I could come back and be myself again. I found over time however, I could never quite be myself again…I was much better. I had proven to myself I could push through any wall, adapt to any challenge and find ways around rocks. I was a survivor, achiever and conqueror.

A Final Word On Quitting

I have never given up on America, nor stopped my love for her no matter how hopeless things have seemed or cynical people become. I believe God has big things in store and wants us to heal, repair, build back and use her for amazing and wonderful things to bless us all and the world.

Honestly, I have no fantasy, dream or wish about living in the White House, being powerful and impressive, or moving to D.C. My vision however is linked simply to my love for God and country, and I actually think I have the ideas and goals that will put us back to where we need and want to be. My ego sure doesn't need it. I want a free, healthy, secure, Christian-influenced country for my kids.

I Have The Right Combination Of Toughness, Discipline And Compassion To Lead

Getting my Ph.D., black belt in Tae Kwon Do, getting BMG distribution, piecing together and hosting my own national TV show and recovering from my near fatal wreck, challenged and developed my core toughness, ability and craving to follow through and achieve. This also developed my strong level of compassion and empathy for others. I realized living and experiencing all these things, the struggles, fatigue and discouragements people go through just trying to stay on track.

When I didn't look right, and felt like dying, I depended on my inner spiritual core and discipline to get out of bed, do my therapy, eye and mouth work again and again. There was no applause and fanfare. I was home alone working, practicing, getting up again and again in our old doublewide. It took two years of hard work and recovery, but I can jog again and do my long hikes with my dogs. I am back.

As your President, I would show you the same combo of weird traits I have to fix, inspire and build up our country. I don't have all the business and political experience so many running will have, but I think I have what this nation needs at this time even more…. REAL vision, humility, compassion, common sense, discipline, morals, toughness and bold ideas to get things done.

Chapter 9
MY VISION FOR AMERICA

We Must Make America Strong Again In Every Way

It is most apparent that President Obama has wanted to bring our nation down and is ashamed of our strength and history. He has acted like a Constitutional shredding machine. Obama has stopped 44 energy projects that have investors, covering oil, nuclear, solar and coal, that simply want to get going. He won't take the time to approve them so they can get moving and help America. That is how much he cares about our energy and independence. Yet, he had the time to give two billion dollars to Brazil to drill for oil, then state to them that we look forward to the day we can import oil from them.

We have a President who tried to enslave America with his medical doctrine and plan that forced health care that the government defined. It manipulated us all to pay for abortions, and rationed care for our seniors, and was peppered with ridiculous controls and taxes.

This President took us to war in Libya, bypassing Congress and going straight to the U.N. This is after our President said in 2007 that the President had no Constitutional authority to engage another nation in an act of war without Congressional approval. He said that it was unconstitutional to do so. This one thing alone is impeachable. He should be politically hung out to dry by his own hypocritical words.

Then there were the 41 czars from hell bypassing congress and acting like an extension of the Obama dictatorship.

How is it that we have a President who is ashamed and apologetic for our country? He should be proud of us and building us up stronger than we already are. America the beautiful is a much needed and rare light on a hill in our world. It has always been the beacon of freedom, hope and opportunity, while offering the divinely inspired miracle of our constitution and bill of rights to all.

As our light has shined and grown in power over our country's historical journey, we have come up against stark and aggressive evil over and over again. We have traditionally known what evil was because of our strong Judeo-Christian heritage, value and worth we have always put on life.

If life and freedom was challenged, we historically have risen to attention and fought to keep it, while also defending others and their rights. Although there will always be complexities and criticisms directed at any war, we fought and led many of the battles against Hitler and in WWII, fought against Imperialistic Japan while later fighting against communism in Korea and Vietnam. We went on to defend Kuwait against an Iraq invasion and stood for freedom in other hot spots around the world. Millions of Americans died protecting these principles and freedoms!

Since 9/11 we have been attacking Al-Qaeda and Islamic Fundamentalist strongholds that train and fund terrorists in Iraq and Afghanistan. We have not only taken down their tyrannical and dangerous regimes, but at our expense (as usual), are rebuilding their country's infrastructure and training their own people to defend and care for themselves. Iraq actually has a chance at life and achievement in the world now, while Afghanistan is on its way to stability and opportunity in time.

What Are The Dangers America Faces Today?

Islamic Fundamentalism

Evil boldly exists and has aggressive agendas today. Islamic Fundamentalism continues in hot pursuit with its goal to put in place a Caliphate and control the world. This is the active, preached about and funded goal by many in the Islamic world today. They are doing a great job throughout Europe and much of the West including the U.S. by training sleeper cells, using our freedoms against us, playing legal games and crying freedom of speech while we naively watch. Now the Middle East is burning down. This is a fight we MUST pay attention to and continue. The only language that will be understood by these Islamic radicals is might and force. Talk certainly won't change their worldview and religious passions of control. They will continue to use silent and violent Jihad to our demise if we let them.

Global Elites Using Economic And Environmental Controls

We have seen for decades those who would destroy our freedom, Christian values and sovereignty from within, namely the global elites, fueled and directed by many in the Trilateral Commission. Their goal has long been to take God out of power and insert a contorted and controlled religion of earth and animal worship, while uniting all religions into a new bastard/Frankenstein child. In this religion there is no accountability to God, only obsession with trumped up environmental rules and regulations while pretending that all religions are the same, Unitarianism. The new God would be government control. It's called sustainability and they want control of our religion, food supply, how we even grow food e.g., backyard gardens, how we work and spend money, our speech, media and land ownership. We are in the increasing stranglehold of these growing controls and diversions now!

The Obama Administration

Whether they admit it or not, Obama and his administration have managed to become the poster child already for a dictatorship and communism. While we sit here thinking this could never happen in our country, Obama and the former House and Senate are systematically doing it.

Reference The Stimulus Package Laced With Precious Government Controls

According to my very reliable banking sources, our major banks were all told by Congress that they had no choice but to take the $5 billion dollar TARP funds, EVEN THOUGH MANY TESTIFIED TO CONGRESS THAT THEY DIDN'T NEED OR WANT THE MONEY. THEY HAD PLENTY OF RESERVES. They were told that all the banks had to take $5 billion each or none could. Of course this small little detail never made it to our media. Amazing how that happens. A few of our banks needed TARP funds but many did not! In my view this was a huge play to manipulate banks into government control while the naïve, American people cheered. We cheered because we were perfectly distracted with our rage against all the bonuses we assumed reflected the whole banking industry, which was the classic lie and setup!! The truth is, that only a few leaders in the banking industry have been corrupt and full of greed, not the masses. This isn't a dictatorial move but rather a government trying to reflect our need for revenge and justice against the financial industry. Steps to tyranny are easier than I thought. We fall quickly for all the tricks and slight of hand.

Take Over The Car Industry

We saw Obama "fire" the CEO of GM, Rick Wagoner. Obama was also demanding Chrysler merge with Fiat if either company is to receive any more money from our Santa Claus government. On what legal grounds does Obama have to order the CEO of GM to be fired? Obviously, the price of receiving money is for Obama's administration to swoop in and control you. That is called a dictatorship, folks.

How Must America Be Strong?

She Must Restore And Draw From Her Christian Heritage Again

We must not apologize for being American or the leader of the free world ever again. We must also build our Judeo-Christian values back up to where they should be, supporting religious speech, behavior and public viewing, starting with Christianity, not ending with it, while in confused, political correctness we promote Islam and its expression. We all make different choices and faiths, but as a nation inspired and built by 95 percent Christians, I frankly resent and have about had it with the idiot, Un-American law suit orgies with the Ten Commandments displays, Memorial Crosses that are to come down, getting 'In God We Trust' off our money, panicking over a birth and manger scene at Christmastime and wearing a cross around your neck in the wrong place at work.

I have a professional and Presidential response to these kind of law suits and behavior. YOU CAN ALL LINE UP AND KISS MY CHRISTIAN AND AMERICAN GRITS!!!

America Must Make Decisions Based On Her Moral Code, Not Oil, Friendship, Or Kiss Up

It doesn't take rocket science to see distortion and manipulation in our response to Saudi Arabia after 9/11 hit. We quickly sent the rest of the Bin Laden's home and started kissing up to the Saudis. Last I checked, 15 of the 19 hijackers were Saudis. As the months unfolded I was most proud of then Governor Giuliani, who chose not to receive the Saudi money gift from one of the royals. He told him where to put it, and that was the right thing to do I felt.

By now, we all know that the Bush family goes back decades in friendship with the Saudi royals and we get oil from them. I think we can all get by now why we were soft on them, though historically they have exported radical Islamist strains of Islam to America and the world. The Wahabi branch of Islam is notorious for its aggressive push, building and financing mosques, Islamic centers and Islamist thinking.

Regardless of what America faces in the months and years ahead, we must quickly become energy independent and put our constitutional backbone back into place so we can reflect our best values and protect our national security. As it is now, we play at it. We poke at it and pretend. It will severely bite us if we don't change our behavior soon in this area.

We Need Economic And Military Strength Again

We can quickly put a big shot of adrenalin into our tilted economy if in 2012 with my proposal of a 2 percent national sales tax and cessation of all other taxes. Though Wall Street and everything else would be taxed at point of purchase, you would have no tax anywhere else. There would be no sneaky, health care tax, road tax, Christmas tax, real estate tax, social security tax or Medicare tax, rat, turtle or bridge tax. Imagine once getting $4,000 a month in your check and only netting $2,800 or so. Can you imagine what you could do with your family if you could actually keep $4,000 a month. Think of businesses not getting hit to steal their profits, and not struggling to make payroll because of high payroll taxes. People could afford to dream again, start businesses again and hire again.

I would also encourage each sovereign state to explore liberating and fair tax plans to stop redundant and unneeded services, and find ways as Governor Walker tried to do with the unions in Wisconsin. States and the federal level have to run business but they must have their service priorities in order. As it is now, we see nothing but an entitlement philosophy, give me, give me, and give me, and Progressive agendas to fund. Meeting budgets with a family on a limited income has never been easy. Nor is it easy at the state or federal level, but it must be done or we all go down in heaping flames.

Military Strength

Ronald Reagan knew the secrets of fabulous government; less Government, lower taxes and regulation and big, healthy military. Our military had to be the strongest on earth. I wholeheartedly believe that. We must make sure with our military budget that they have all they need to maintain, treat our troops right during active duty and after, and develop the best equipment and technology possible. I would propose with our 8 trillion dollar wallet (remembering that $3.5 trillion is debt pay down) that we put another $100 billion into our military to secure them and our country in every way needed. This would include putting in place $100 million each year to pay rent and/or mortgage of active duty personnel while they are on active duty overseas and two years after their return so they can readjust. Though there is a law on the books to keep banks from foreclosing on the homes of active duty personnel, it has been done by greedy banks one too many times. That makes me MORE than grumpy. In fact, it makes me want to become President just to fix this nightmare for starters.

Finally, regarding our military might and strength, we must secure and continue to build our nuclear strength, not stupidly undo it as Obama has tried to do by signing the START treaty with Russia. Strength with the right attitude is what we need, not weakness with the wrong attitude. I would do everything within my power to undo this treaty.

Encourage Manufacturing And Industry To Come On Home

I am the first to understand that businesses and corporations need to make a profit in order to survive. That is why over many decades now, many have gone overseas to operate. Our country has slammed what I call the "Unholy Trinity" down their throats; taxation, litigation and regulation. Of course we need guidelines and common sense regulations with business, but when extreme environmentalism and socialist agendas start forcing micro controls, fines and expenses just to exist as a business, people and companies either go bankrupt, they quit or go overseas.

It is critical to dramatically pull back the manipulative orgy of regulations and controls so that our nuclear, natural gas, oil and other energy sources can actually and quickly develop and create the energy

America needs. All other businesses and corporations also need to know that America is the place to produce their wares again and employ our citizens first. To encourage this further, I would make sure U.S. products made in the U.S. were not taxed, but products being sold to us from other countries did have a tax coming in.

We Need Our Nation Debt Free

This is a must-have goal for anyone who becomes President. If you had $3.5-4 trillion a year to chunk it down we would be completely out of debt in 4-6 years. What would that do to the value of our dollar and commerce worldwide? I want to see that, don't you?

Encourage Freedom Here And Abroad

The first thing we must do in America is to model our freedom based on and reflecting our Constitution, Declaration of Independence and Judeo-Christian values. Our current President says our Constitution is flawed. That is another "Kiss my grits moment."

Our founding documents and Christian core is unique in the entire world. We must continue to be a light on a hill for freedom and Christian values. We are it. God and the world are counting on us and so are our children. Evil is organized and continues to boldly rise up like a Cobra to strike us. We have faced the Imperialist agenda of Japan in WWII, the Nazis, Communism and now fundamentalist and radical Islam who wants to enslave and take over the world.

We can stand for REAL freedom only if we hold on to the God of the Holy Bible for our strength, and leading while having the guts to stand up to defined evil, not be intimidated by it, distracted by it or influenced by it. Radical Islam is evil and dangerous and must be challenged, defined and stopped in every way possible.

Chapter 10
WHY OBAMA SHOULD BE THROWN OUT IN 2012

Let's cut to the bottom line, shall we? We have a man in the White House who revealed who he was and what he would do long before he was elected President. He had already demonstrated that he was a radical Leftist, and what his change for America would be if we gave him power. The U.S. gave him power, now we are reaping the consequences and must have a bold and clear plan to get him out of office before he completely destroys our country.

Let's look at what has inspired Obama and his socialist/communist behavior. Read his own books and that will tell you plenty about his own racism and belief in colonial Imperialism. In his book, *Dreams From My Father,* which most believe was penned by William Ayers, and not Obama, he talks of his alleged father an "anti-colonial" activist, also named Barack Hussein Obama. He believed in classic redistribution of wealth. His idea was that any wealthy country could have only obtained their wealth by stealing from poor people so that justified taking their wealth by any means necessary and redistributing it. That is the clear philosophy of father and son.

Mr. "pull people together" Obama, also had a few things to say about race in his book. While he and the Progressive democrats have been calling us all racists for daring to confront his unconstitutional and Anti-American behavior, the real racist and flamethrower has been Obama himself. Just a few juicy quotes from *Dreams From My Father:*

"I ceased to advertise my mother's race at the age of 12 or 13, when I began to suspect that by doing so I was ingratiating myself to whites." Obama continues his openness: "I found a solace in nursing a pervasive sense of grievance and animosity against my mother's race." "There was something about him that made me wary, a little too sure of himself, maybe. And white." A final taste of race enlightenment: "I never emulate white men and brown men whose fates didn't speak to my own. It was into my father's image, the black man, son of Africa, that I'd packed all the attributes I sought in myself, the attributes of Martin and Malcolm, Dubois and Mandela."

As Obama embraced his adult life, he surrounded himself with radicals from Reverend Wright who preached hatred and anger against America, to William Ayers, former terrorist with the Weather Underground. There was a sea of other radical, Anti-American and antisemitic people Obama surrounded himself with then, and continues today with his czars. Never before have we seen a President who has appointed 41 czars who completely bypassed Congress and answer directly to Obama. This gives our President too much power and makes them an extension of a dictatorship. Our longest serving Senator ever, Democrat Robert Byrd, was boldly on record before he passed away, criticizing President Obama for these appointments of czars because it wipes out our system of checks and balances. I couldn't agree more.

The House continues to battle the czar distortion. They passed an amendment (No. 204), eliminating funding for President Obama's czars.

By now you have heard that Obama taught ACORN workers from Saul Alinsky's book ***Rules For Radicals***, a book by the way, which was dedicated to Lucifer inside the front cover. Shall we sing a hymn now? Alinsky was a piece of work and was considered the "father of modern American radicalism." He said things like "Keep your friends close, keep your enemies closer." He talked all about playing dirty, spying, anti-corporate activism, brutal tactics and severely damaging people's reputations. These are just a few of the concepts that Obama taught to ACORN workers that represented his real beliefs.

As Obama was running for office, the country knew of his radical and leftist voting record as a Senator, not only voting for every pro-abortion bill he could, but also infanticide. There weren't enough abortion bills for Obama apparently, so he had to vote for letting the baby die without receiving medical care that actually survived an abortion.

It also came out before Obama was elected, his ties with Weather Underground terrorist, William Ayers. I know, I broke the story on the national scene, with a published article and on my show, Good Friday of 2008. I had been called with that information at my home, by a former Pentagon and C.I.A. person. I am humbled to say I was nominated for the coveted Ronald Reagan award given out by CPAC each year for breaking it on my show. Finally, Sean Hannity started talking about the William Ayers link with Obama, but precious few others.

Horrifyingly, the nation was stuck on stupid and taken in by Obama's looks and color. Surely he would be another Martin Luther King or John F. Kennedy. Try, Castro, Chavez, Mussolini, Hitler and Zelaya. That would be much closer to what we have regardless of what color or race he is.

What Did Obama Do When Elected?

Our country was and has been trying to recover from a severe recession as he has spent several trillion dollars and rolled out stimulus this and that. During this type of national stress and reality, Obama reversed Bush's Mexico City policy, which now meant we would be paying for birth control and abortions all over the world, not just in the U.S. He also spent $900 million almost the moment he walked into the oval office to give to the terrorist Muslim group, HAMAS. This is the peace-loving group that chronically and constantly attacks our best ally in the Middle East, Israel.

Then Came The Big One – The Health Care Plan From Hell

Obama started in on his expensive crusade to push his health care plan. With the help of his then progressive left congress it was voted in. He lied to America the entire time he was presenting his health care plan. "We could keep our own health insurance." "We wouldn't be paying for abortions." "There wouldn't be death panels." "Health care costs and insurance prices would go down." I could fill up a book just on the endless manipulation, sound bite/Saul Alinsky theatre, and lies shoved down American's throats regarding this bill. As you already know, unless you are dead, there really are death panels, and forced end of life counseling for seniors every year when they go in for a wellness visit. We really are forced to pay for abortions whether we want to or not. We are forced to have government-approved health insurance, or receive fines. Earlier on in the battle before it was put into law, there was going to be jail time also. There are tons of not so hidden taxes peppered all through this bill. Even worse, the care is decided by the government and rationed, using age and cost as a health care decider, not quality care. This bill in my view after analyzing it would have made Dr. Mengele happy in Nazi Germany. Let this bill die a painful, quick and cruel death.

Thankfully, this part of Obama's troubling legacy is on the skids with the Conservative House now in the process of defunding and dismembering it. The new congress voted to repeal it but as expected the leftist-controlled Senate wouldn't back it. We also have two federal judges who have declared it unconstitutional. Judge Vincent, the second judge to rule, also represented 26 states that are planning to fight it.

Obama Started A War In Libya – Why?

In March 2011, out of nowhere Obama had gone to the U.N., then launched us into a war working with the French and British against Gadhafi in Libya. We don't get oil from Libya and they weren't an enemy to America. There have been atrocities and attacks on those who have marched for freedom all over the Middle East, Syria, Egypt, Iran, Jordan, Tunisia and more. Why was Libya the big war to have now?

This has cost us $100 million a day as we lobbed hundreds of missiles into Libya and no one seemed to be in control. Then we were told by the time $600 million had been spent, in just a few days, that NATO was in control. We heard the manipulative speech from Obama saying that it wouldn't have been American to avoid attacking Libya. Obama didn't want to see a ton of body bags before America acted. Of course, with all his saintly, human rights motives, he hadn't bothered to even approach Congress, only the U.N. This is most interesting, since he is on record saying in 2007 that a U.S.

President had no constitutional authority to engage another nation in an act of war without Congressional approval or oversight. That is exactly what Obama did. He should be impeached on this breach alone by his own words.

This isn't fringe and a waste of GOP time. This has been and is a national emergency and if I was running for President, I WOULD SURE ADDRESS IT IN MY CAMPAIGN AND IN ANY MEDIA DEBATE OR EVENT.

What do we see as Obama's legacy: He has apologized non stop for our country, fought against energy independence, while funding oil for Brazil, forced nationally controlled and rationed health care down our throat, called conservatives and Tea Party folks names non-stop, stood for the building of a mosque at Ground Zero in New York, bowed down to the Saudi Muslim King, lead us into a war with Libya not approved by congress, spent trillions of dollars we don't have, increased our out of control debt and raised to our taxes, while creating an extension to his dictatorship, bypassing congress, his 41 czars.

Regardless as to whether you believe I am the one to take on Obama and the GOP machine, please don't vote for Obama again if you love freedom, our constitution and country. It never was about his race. It is about our constitution, freedom, Judeo-Christian values and way of life.

Also, it is not about Republicans or Democrats, liberals or conservatives, red states or blue states. It is about being truly American, and red, white and blue states. The assaults, name-calling and slander, continues against those who dare to question and make comments about Obama's eligibility and constitutional status to be President.

We are distractions and we are racist, conspiratorial Birthers. Let us look at some of the messiah-level conservatives and what they have to say about this. First on our list of "on high" opinions is Karl Rove, a Fox News contributor and the former Senior Advisor and Deputy Chief of Staff under George W. Bush. I have respected and supported much of what he has said over the years, but he loses my respect and support on this issue. He said on Bill O'Reilly that the Republican Party has to focus on real issues, not "non-issues." The party should ignore the "Birther" movement. Rove compared the Birthers to the John Birch Society, a far-right group started in the 1950s. He compared the 9/11 deniers with the Birthers, those who want Obama to prove his eligibility.

Rove made these comments to an agreeing Bill O'Reilly who also has marginalized and insulted "Birthers" for the last two years (Translation: A Birther is anyone who looks at the sea of growing evidence that Obama was not born in Hawaii, and wants him to come clean and show his long form birth certificate.) Karl Rove was advising the GOP not to waste time on this "non-issue," and certainly not give anyone who believes that way any profile or stature in the party. Worshiping and sold out Bill O'Reilly, agreed.

Other Conservative Big Dogs Who Know Better

Glenn Beck has put down and minimalized the eligibility issue all along. He had done this while talking passionately about our Constitution, Founding Fathers, waging war against George Soros and more. Recently on the ***Peter Boyle Show*** he was asked about eligibility. I was interviewed myself on the ***Peter Boyle Show***, and he rocks. Glenn is reported to have said the following, "Where he

was born? I don't know." Then later, "He cares about the U.S. Constitution."   He went on…"Our rights are being violated right now
and I want to concentrate on that." OK, Glenn, ignore the "rights
violating elephants" stampeding through the room! So far we are
wasting time representing a non-issue according to Karl Rove and
Glenn. Think we should be focusing on our rights being violated,
not the eligibility issue?

Who Else Has Conservative Wisdom To Add To This List?

Even the amazing Sarah Palin has strangely minimized this
issue. She has stated on her Facebook postings: "At no point, not
during the campaign, and not during recent interviews, have I asked
the President to produce his birth certificate or suggested that he
was not born in the United States." Why, Sarah, did you not ever
suggest Obama come clean with this and show his birth certificate?
You act as if that is a great thing that you didn't ask Obama to show
he was born in the U.S. I think it is a shame and missing the mark
that you didn't.

Do you not think it odd that John McCain was asked to show
his birth certificate to the media and left…he did. Obama has been
asked, sued and begged to show his long form birth certificate and
he has answered by spending over two million dollars hiding every
record he has, while calling us names. According to a recent poll
over 51 percent of Americans don't believe he was born in the U.S.
It is RATHER a big question mark.

Regardless of all the suspicious behavior by Obama, fingers
and signed affidavits pointing him to being born in Kenya www.
obamacrimes.com, and even a former election official, Tim Adams

of Hawaii, signing an affidavit in 2008 saying Obama was not born in Hawaii, Rove, Beck, Palin continue to ignore and betray this issue. Isn't it most interesting that they all appear on Fox regularly and they either have their own shows or are regular guests? One thing is for sure. They refuse to honestly deal with this glaring issue of national concern and danger. Can you say, threats, intimidation, bribes and payoffs?? I think someone controlling and/or running Fox got to them and they are scared.

How is it that even with Dr. Jerry Corsi, the Governor of Hawaii, Neil Abercrombie, and former election official, Tim Adams saying the birth certificate is not there, that the real story continues to be buried in most of radio and TV in America?? OBAMA LIED ABOUT WHERE HE WAS BORN. That is the real story. People don't lie and spend money to hide information unless they have something to lose.

This isn't fringe and a waste of GOP time. This has been and is a national emergency and if I was running for President, I WOULD SURE ADDRESS IT IN MY CAMPAIGN AND IN ANY MEDIA DEBATE OR EVENT. www.thepeoplespresident.me.

Can we do it? I hope I haven't misled you while sharing all my ideas and passions for my country. I am only too aware how imperfect I am in every way. Ask my husband, parents, kids and my closest friends, they will tell you plenty.

I do stand here as one of you, flaws and all, and I will commit to serving our agenda. I say in bold and believing faith that together we will do the following:

* Bring freedom back to America

* Get America completely out of debt and never allow that to happen again

* Restore our Judeo-Christian values on every level

* Stand boldly against Islamic radicalism and the international abuse of Sharia law

* Create total energy independence

* Restore American exceptionalism, manufacturing and industry again

* Explore real health care reforms that protect competition, choices and prices for all

* Look for creative and real ways to improve America, attack poverty and crime.

*Restore our international reputation again by being ourselves, becoming stronger, demonstrating compassion, and approaching problem solving with common sense.

* Honor the other branches of government, especially when it comes to the potential of a war.

* Stop sending billions of dollars to the middle east and elsewhere that long ago became kiss up.

Together Let Us Show That Freedom Still Exists In America. The People's President: Of The People, By The People, For The People. Bring It On!

Let's get America back, talk REAL issues, liberate ourselves and our country.

Join me in several ways:
I need volunteers in all 50 states to get the word out about my campaign and race for the Presidency. This is a grass roots campaign and together we can get it done.
If a million folks wanting the kind of America I am envisioning would click on the PayPal button at www.laurieroth2012.com and give just $10.00 per month (a Starbucks coffee and doughnut), and agree to share my campaign message and challenge with 10 more people, we would saturate the country, have all the signatures we need to get on the ballot, and last but not least...

HAVE A REAL CHANCE TO GO ALL THE WAY TO THE WHITE HOUSE.

Go to www.laurieroth2012.com, and find out where I will be making appearances and doing book signings, how you can help in your state and what needs to be done. We have easy steps and guidelines for you at the website.
Contribute $10.00. Find 10 more friends who can do the same. Thank you.
Some of you can contribute $1,000 or the maximum $2,500 per person. Find 10 more friends who can do the same and keep it going.
If you don't want another person in the White House who is

funded by massive corporations, global elitists, and "mystery
money," we will all have to work together; volunteer by
volunteer and dollar by dollar.

Join me each day on my national radio show www.therothshow.
com from 3-6pm PST. Call in and let me know what you think.
You can listen online or catch the archive later if you can't listen
yet on a station near you. Better yet, if I'm not airing on your
talk station, call them and tell them you want my show to air.

Let's bring it on!

CPSIA information can be obtained at www.ICGtesting.com
Printed in the USA
BVOW021146081111

275578BV00001B/114/P